YOU ARE THE CATHOLIC BRAND

MATTHEW KILMURRY

Matthew Kilmurry has been at the forefront of the efforts of the Church to move its communication into the digital age. Matthew's heart is deeply rooted in his Catholic faith, something that is branded on his soul. The uniting of his faith and his experience in creating brands has brought forth *You Are the Catholic Brand*, a wonderful book on how to communicate the good news in a digital age.

—Most Rev. Christopher Coyne, bishop of Burlington (VT) and chair of the Committee on Communications, United States Conference of Catholic Bishops (USCCB)

Matthew Kilmurry has done the impossible: He has combined the lessons of marketing with the demands of the new evangelization, creating an absorbing guide for all Catholics who want to spread the good news of our faith but are unsure how. With unflinching honesty, Kilmurry draws lessons from his own personal experiences and successful marketing career, giving practical suggestions to help even the shyest of disciples accompany, encounter, and change all those we come in contact with, starting with ourselves.

—Greg Erlandson, author, editor, and publishing executive

Beautifully written and exceptionally real, *You Are the Catholic Brand* provides practical ways to offer others an encounter with Christ and his Church while deepening personal faith. Matthew Kilmurry shows clearly how evangelization starts with a creative and courageous invitation by the Holy Spirit and us.

—Rev. Frank Donio, SAC, director, Catholic Apostolate Center, Washington, DC

Readers Rave About

You Are the Catholic Brand

You Are the Catholic Brand is a timely, inviting, and engaging
help for those who want to live life with more purpose and
highlight their brand as a disciple to their spouse, parent, friend,
coworker, or neighbor. Drawing from life experience, Matthew
Kilmurry offers a guide to building a relationship with God,
overcoming personal weakness, and discovering the mission God
has for you.

—Donald Cardinal Wuerl, archbishop of Washington, DC

The practical advice in Matthew's book comes at the perfect
time, when so many people seek a greater understanding of their
Catholic identity. His real-life examples and encouragement help
us, the body of Christ, articulate a greater purpose for our lives
and rise to the challenge of being more courageous and authentic
witnesses to the faith.

—Jennifer Baugh, founder and executive director of
Young Catholic Professionals, a national nonprofit organization
inspiring young professionals "to Work in Witness for Christ"

Christianity, and sharing the good news, depends on Christians.
That's right: YOU! Matthew's book reminds us of the essential
truth about living our faith loudly, proudly, and effectively. We
all need to work on our brand of faith—not by wearing it on our
sleeves but by living it out from our hearts. This book can help
the average Catholic to become an extraordinary evangelizer.

—Rev. Leo E. Patalinghug, author, speaker,
television and radio host; see him at GraceBeforeMeals.com

You Are the Catholic Brand is a wonderful teaching resource for parish leaders and others in ministry, as well as an invitation to the faithful to see how to evangelize. How we share our own experiences as Catholics and how we communicate the importance of the Catholic faith in building a personal relationship with Jesus is directly related to our success in helping others to better know Jesus through the Church. Matthew Kilmurry expertly melds marketing and evangelization in this unique guide that I pray will help the faithful answer God's call to spread the good news to all nations.

—Most Rev. William E. Lori, archbishop of Baltimore

Matthew Kilmurry invites us to brand training about our faith. Speaking from the intersection of faith and consumer culture, *You Are the Catholic Brand* is an enthusiastic, interesting, and accessible take on evangelization. I appreciate it for helping us to read the signs of the times.

—Daniella Zsupan-Jerome, PhD, professor of pastoral theology, Notre Dame Seminary Graduate School of Theology, consultant to the USCCB's Communications Office, and author of *Connected Toward Communion*

Matthew Kilmurry is a fresh and engaging new voice within the Catholic world. In his book, readers are afforded a penetrating look into Kilmurry's marketing mind as he effectively enables you to share your love for Christ and his Church with a hungry world. This is a smartly conceived book that will certainly reshape the way people present their faith to the world.

—Kevin Wells, former sportswriter, speaker, and best-selling author of *Burst: A Story of God's Grace When Life Falls Apart*

Bravo, Matthew, for summarizing succinctly, powerfully, vividly, and hopefully the role and mission of Christians today. Pope Francis says Christianity is an encounter with Jesus that brings us to others. Matthew understands the urgent need of this encounter very well and will help you understand it, too. I highly recommend this book to pastors, evangelists, lay leaders, youth ministers, university chaplains, and serious Catholics who are trying to dialogue with the world around us. It is a breath of pure oxygen.

—Rev. Thomas Rosica, CSB, CEO, Salt and Light Catholic Media Foundation, English-language attaché, Holy See Press Office

Matthew Kilmurry articulates a fresh vision of the good news of Jesus Christ. His voice is authentic and moving as he witnesses to the love and power of Christ and also encourages us to witness with intention and passion.

—Sr. Theresa Rickard, OP, DMin, president and executive director, RENEW International

As Catholics, we are privileged to be spokespersons for the most life-changing product the world has ever seen: the gospel. With humor and depth, Kilmurry will help Catholics of any age share their faith more confidently, effectively, and with greater impact.

—Rev. Michael White, pastor of the Church of the Nativity, Timonium, MD, and coauthor of the best-selling book *Rebuilt*

I'm a sinner. You're probably a sinner, too. And for sinners like us, the thought of representing Catholicism to the world isn't just scary—it seems like the ultimate spiritual joke! But in this book, Matthew Kilmurry shows us how to represent and pass along our faith. It's our job as Catholics, whether we're ready or not.

—Lino Rulli, *The Catholic Guy* (Sirius XM Satellite Radio), author of *Sinner* and *Saint*

YOU ARE THE
CATHOLIC
B R A N D

MATTHEW
KILMURRY

Liguori

Imprimi Potest:
Stephen T. Rehrauer, CSsR, Provincial
Denver Province, the Redemptorists

Published by Liguori Publications
Liguori, Missouri 63057

To order, visit Liguori.org or call 800-325-9521.

Library of Congress Cataloging-in-Publication Data

Names: Kilmurry, Matthew, author
Title: You Are the Catholic Brand / Matthew Kilmurry
Description: First Edition I Liguori: Liguori Publications, 2016
Identifiers: LCCN 2016023368 I ISBN 9780764826412
Subjects: LCSH: Christian life–Catholic authors I Catholics I
  Advertising–Religious aspects–Catholic Church I
  Ambassadors–Miscellanea
Classification: LCC BX2350.3 .K54 2016 I DDC 248.4/82–dc23
LC record available at https://lccn.loc.gov/2016023368

Liguori Publications, a nonprofit corporation, is an apostolate of the Redemptorists. To learn more about the Redemptorists, visit Redemptorists.com.

Printed in the United States of America
20 19 18 17 16 / 5 4 3 2 1
First Edition

Interior design: Wendy Barnes

Contents

THE MOST POWERFUL MARKETING TOOL THE
CATHOLIC CHURCH HAS IS YOU.

For Jennifer Brinker.
Friend, godmother, and master of the red pen.

Introduction

You represent the Catholic Christian brand to everyone you meet. We often believe that's solely the responsibility of those living religious life (the pope, bishops, priests, deacons, sisters, and brothers). But in reality, the Catholic brand also belongs to lay Catholics who live, work, and play in the world outside the Church. You have been given tremendous power as a Catholic, and whether you know it or not, you are wielding that power at all times. There is no "off" button. Your influence is always "on" even if you don't feel like a good Catholic.

I am convinced that everyday Catholics have no idea how important they are and how much they impact the Catholic brand each day. It is the mission of this book to help all Catholics in the United States see with a new lens how much they influence the Catholic brand, and to give them tools to wield that power for the glory of God. This book is for all Catholics no matter where you are in your journey. Get ready. Your faith, your personal Catholic brand, will never be the same.

Achieving, managing, and growing a brand is a concept now

accepted by both CEOs and checkout counter clerks alike. Brands have exploded on the scene and have become the watchword for our consumer culture. You can easily think of dozens of brands that are a part of your daily life. Many of us display them with pride on our clothes and the cars we drive.

There may be no brand that has had more negative press than the Catholic Church. We hear the accusations all the time: persecution, wars, sexual abuse. Some of this press is true and the criticism well deserved. But some of it is false or a distorted view of the truth. This book does not suggest ways to fix the world's view of the institutional Church; instead, it focuses on something more manageable—and more important. You.

Every time we receive the holy Eucharist, we become a walking tabernacle. You may be the only tabernacle someone ever comes into contact with. It's a wonderful privilege and offers fantastic opportunities for evangelization, compassion, and mercy.

Over the last hundred years, companies have started to understand the benefits of creating a brand, something we as Catholics have known for two thousand years. Companies spend years researching and boatloads of money defining themselves. One of the most important aspects of creating a brand is developing a mission statement, a short, concise statement on what the company believes and how it plans on accomplishing its mission. Sound familiar? As Catholics, we recite something similar anytime we say the Creed. Just as companies need employees to buy into the brand with enthusiasm and a willingness to live out the brand in their daily work lives, so does the Catholic Church. If the employees don't buy into the brand, it falls flat.

But be encouraged! Unlike employees in a company who get just one day of brand training during orientation, Catholics have some of the most time-tested training material ever created. In addition, we have a helper, the Holy Spirit, who gives us the strength, knowledge, and power to be who God intended us to be. All we have to do is be willing. If only all jobs came with supernatural help like that!

So, as Catholics, what can we learn from brands? First, it's important to note that brands have always been around. There is no person or organization that comes close to the success achieved by Jesus and the Catholic Church he established.

Just look at the Church's presence in today's world. There is a folktale that Napoleon once bragged to a French cardinal that he would destroy the Church. The wise and unintimidated cardinal responded, "Good luck. We've been trying to do that for centuries."

But Christianity isn't merely a brand, it's a religion. People don't turn their lives over to brands directly. As my former boss said, a brand is a "gut feeling." A brand consists of things you've learned throughout your life: thoughts, pictures and colors, statistics, experiences you've both had and not had, smells and tastes, comforts, speeches, and everything else wrapped into a single emotional experience. As humans, we can't process all those individual pieces at once when we're making a decision. As a result, our minds compensate by giving us a lifetime summary that enables us to say yes or no. We make the vast majority of our decisions through these gut feelings.

The Roman Catholic Church represents an archetype brand. Here in America, the U.S. Conference of Catholic Bishops and many other organizations work hard to create positive, Catholic centric brand messages. Yet, the Church holds its core values given by God, not to an institution–though the institution of the Church is vital in continuing to uphold those values–but to the individuals who accept the gift of faith. It is an organization in which the people make the brand rather than the brand making the people.

The only people capable of improving the Catholic brand are individual Catholics, not just bishops and priests but also lay leaders and the working faithful. Corporations quickly learned the importance of individuals in marketing. Despite billions spent on advertising, a top-down approach only works until that first bad personal experience.

However, a positive experience can do more for a brand than billions of dollars in advertising. For example, the first time I heard of Jos. A. Banks, they were having a "buy one suit, get two free" sale.

I had just taken a job where I would need to wear a suit every day. It was perfect timing. The employees who helped me were very friendly. They took time to ask about my suit wearing history and my upcoming needs. They showed me suit and shirt options that could be mixed and matched to maximize my purchase, so that three outfits could extend over five days. I was thrilled!

Two months later, I ended up ripping the sleeve of my suit jacket. I wasn't sure if I could get a replacement jacket or not, but thought it was worth going back to check. I thought they might even have replacement sleeves to repair the jacket. Despite how crazy it sounded, I went back and asked if there was a way to replace just the arm. The employee took my coat and disappeared in the back to talk to the tailor. Five minutes later he returned with a brand new suit. "Do you have a dollar?" he asked. "Yeah," I mumbled, dumbfounded. "I'll need it to put a transaction in the computer," he said.

It took me a moment to realize I was getting a completely new suit for one dollar, two whole months after my original purchase.

Like 99 percent of businessmen wearing suits, I don't really know the difference between the material, the cut, or the stitching. I only know three things about suits: how they feel, how they fit, and the experience I have purchasing it. This experience made me a Jos. A. Banks customer forever.

In the same light, the Catholic Church is a large umbrella sheltering a myriad of experiences of faith. Everyone from saints to sinners, charismatics to traditionalists, apologists to social justice workers, finds emotional experiences that keep them coming back to the Church. These variations are different, complementary expressions of the one true faith. If we want to continue bringing Catholics home or converts into the Church, we have to provide great "customer service" that keeps our friends, family, and acquaintances coming back.

We are all spokespersons for the Catholic brand whether we intend to be or not. Following these six simple steps, which will be explained in more detail in the following chapters, will help you more effectively communicate your Catholic brand.

1. BE CONVERTED ANEW.

2. KNOW WHAT TYPE OF CATHOLIC YOU ARE AND GET ENTHUSIASTIC ABOUT IT.

3. KNOW YOUR CUSTOMERS.

4. PERSONALIZE YOUR MESSAGES.

5. MEASURE YOUR RETURN ON INVESTMENT.

6. MAINTAIN YOUR BRAND.

Chapter
One

Be Converted Anew

Become the type of customer
every company dreams about.

Sunblock has been the bane of the Kilmurry family vacation for as long as we've had kids. With six small children, we go through it like water. Inevitably, someone gets sunburned or they cry and wipe their eyes and then cry some more because it stings. Our family finally took to the Internet in search of a solution, where we came across an Australian sunblock called **Blue Lizard**. This sunblock was everything it claimed to be. It only needed to be applied once, and the stinging eyes were gone.

We soon converted from customers to Brand Evangelists. We touted the awesomeness of this sunblock to anyone willing to listen on a hot, sunny day. We converted a few of our friends by offering to make bulk orders so everyone could save on shipping. We became the type of customers every company dreams about. We probably talked with greater ease and enthusiasm about this sunblock than our amazing experiences with Jesus and his Church. How many of us can think of a product we evangelize with more enthusiasm than our faith?

Brand Evangelist

"Brand Evangelist" is a term currently circulating through the business world. It's corporate jargon that refers to customers so in love with the brand, they do unofficial marketing for it. Businesses have shifted focus from creating new customers to activating Brand Evangelists and giving them the tools to do marketing for the company.

This kind of marketing is believable too, because it's compounded by a hundred or a thousand Brand Evangelists. There is nothing more powerful. Who hasn't encountered a passionate fan of a movie, car, restaurant, or band? Their enthusiasm is contagious. Through those fans you live a transformational experience, the moment they took a bite of the best pizza in the world, how the car felt as they turned a sharp corner, or a movie that left them speechless. All you need is the look on their face. Those rational details like ingredients in the pizza sauce, the car's suspension system, or the technical details of the movie's production aren't irrelevant, but they don't have the impact of that emotional connection.

The experience created an emotion for the Brand Evangelist that is attractive to others, and that is what emotional marketing is all about. It's the promise of an unforgettable experience. This is true in our spiritual lives also. Those of us who are converts often feel unequipped to pass along the faith because we don't always know the details of our faith like the exact Scripture quotes for a given situation or the accurate historical accounts. We are left paralyzed. But just as the Brand Evangelist doesn't know the ingredients of the pizza sauce or the car's suspension, we have to remember that all those details about the faith aren't the only thing people are attracted to. People are looking for an unforgettable experience. They're looking for conversion.

EMOTIONAL MARKETING IS THE PROMISE OF AN UNFORGETTABLE EXPERIENCE.

Whether your conversion happened in a flash of lightning or a slow progression, it is time to be converted anew. Pope Francis compels all of us to do so in the opening of his first apostolic exhortation, *Evangelii Gaudium*:

> I invite all Christians, everywhere, at this very moment, to a renewed personal encounter with Jesus Christ, or at least an openness to letting him encounter them; I ask all of you to do this unfailingly each day. No one should think that this invitation is not meant for him or her, since "no one is excluded from the joy brought by the Lord." The Lord does not disappoint those

who take this risk; whenever we take a step towards Jesus, we come to realize that he is already there, waiting for us with open arms. Now is the time to say to Jesus: "Lord, I have let myself be deceived; in a thousand ways I have shunned your love, yet here I am once more, to renew my covenant with you. I need you. Save me once again, Lord, take me once more into your redeeming embrace." (Paragraph 3)

The single biggest choice we have in this life is one that requires setting aside faith in ourselves and believing in something greater. We are called to answer the question Jesus asked his disciples, "Who do *you* say that I am?" This is historically referred to as the *Kerygma*, the basic presentation of the life, death, and resurrection of Jesus Christ.

When the restaurant chain **Friday's** went through a major re-brand, they required that all employees go through the brand training again, even if they had been employed for many years. The reasoning was that it's always a good idea to review what makes a brand special. That's exactly what Pope Francis, our "CEO," is calling Catholics to do. Our brand training is a personal encounter with Jesus Christ. But when Pope Francis suggests this encounter, what does he mean? Unlike a corporate brand that wants everyone to share the same perspective, Catholics develop different answers to the question "Who do you say that I am?" just as Jesus did when he asked his disciples. Each person should have an unique perspective on his or her conversion to Christ and a unique perspective on who Christ is.

As you consider the question "Who do you say that I am?" think in terms of a problem and a solution. Write it down. What problem does Jesus solve for you? What solution does he offer you? The answer

WHAT PROBLEM DOES JESUS SOLVE FOR YOU AND HOW?

to these questions is deeply personal. We don't worship Jesus because he was a great teacher. There are thousands of those throughout history. Jesus is personal to each of us. He knows our deepest desires, fears, and sufferings and walks with us.

Below is my response to this question. Based on my background, it's not surprising that evangelical thinking has influenced me. Perhaps yours is based more on historical facts, miracles you've witnessed, the power of prayer, influence from family...

Problem

Heaven is perfect and nothing imperfect can enter it. God is just and he will not let one crime—one sin—go unpunished.

> *Be assured, the wicked shall not go unpunished,*
> *but the offspring of the just shall escape.*
> *(Proverbs 11:21)*

Since we have all sinned, none of us deserve heaven.

> *There is no one just, not one. (Romans 3:10)*

We were kicked out of paradise once for eating the forbidden fruit (original sin) and humanity had yet to produce a single sin-free, rational adult who could walk right into heaven. Unless God did something about it, we were bound to remain separated from him forever.

Solution

You were dead in your transgressions and sins. (Ephesians 2:1)

Then God did the unthinkable, something no Hollywood writer could ever dream up. God became a man and took out his perfect judgment on himself.

For God so loved the world that he gave his only
Son, so that everyone who believes in him might not
perish but might have eternal life. (John 3:16)

Jesus is the spotless lamb. He is the perfect sacrifice once and for all. Old Testament Jews would have understood this well. Prior to Jesus, sins were repeatedly covered up by the blood of an animal sacrifice.

How do I know Jesus's blood is for me? If we are Christians who endure to the end, we are covered up by the blood of the one sufficient sacrifice. When we enter the afterlife to be judged, God will look upon us and see his Son. We may still need to be purified in purgatory before we're ready to join God in heaven, but everyone who goes to purgatory is on their way to heaven.

How do we get to heaven? We can't earn it. As St. Paul wrote, "For by grace you have been saved through faith, and this is not from you; it is the gift of God; it is not from works, so no one may boast" (Ephesians 2:8–9). What we do have to do is repent, believe, be baptized, and live a life that reflects our faith.

TRY THE SAME THING WITH YOUR PROBLEM AND SOLUTION.

This kind of belief isn't easy. **It's a dirt-under-your-fingernails, head-on-the-pillow-exhausted, self-dying, relentless kind of belief.** We have to show God we believe in his Son, and that requires action. Jesus said those who call his name out loud but refuse to help those in need never really knew him.

Many will say to me on that day, 'Lord, Lord, did we not prophesy in your name? Did we not drive out demons in your name? Did we not do mighty deeds in your name?'

Then I will declare to them solemnly, 'I never knew you. Depart from me, you evildoers.'
(Matthew 7:22–23)

God knows us too well. Anything less than true faith demonstrated through our actions is mere lip service.

✳ ✳ ✳

Our conversion is the foundation of being a Catholic Christian Brand Evangelist, but the momentum cannot end there. To be effective Brand Evangelists, conversion must lead to something else very important: **credibility**.

Skeptical consumers aren't new. Wary of being sold "a bill of goods," skepticism was personified in the great American Broadway hit, *The Music Man*, which tells the story of a traveling salesman who gains the trust of everyone in a small town and then cashes in his credibility selling them something he doesn't have (namely music lessons). Growing up I took part in the musical as one of the town children. I only had one line, but the play left an impression on me. I told myself *I* would never fall for a conman like that. But the truth is, no matter how we tell ourselves we won't, we all fall for cons. The reason is misplaced credibility. Everyone has a credibility filter and we use it hundreds of times every day. Especially in today's culture, we are bombarded by so many facts, figures, statements, and offerings that we could never explore the merits of each before deciding whether

CONVERSION MUST LEAD TO CREDIBILITY.

or not to accept that information as true or false, bad or good. We may be under the illusion that our credibility filter works the majority of the time due to a lifetime of critical thinking. But, let me tell you, it is incredibly easy to manipulate. One example of ways brands get past your filter is through the use of celebrity spokespeople.

Through whatever has fueled their fame (acting, sporting achievements, and so on), celebrities have a much better chance of moving through your credibility filter. When we watch them play a favorite character, we experience highs and lows with them. When we spend the season rooting for them, we begin to feel comradery. We feel like we actually know them. These celebrities become part of our lives and we begin to trust them.

When a brand is doing mass marketing through television or radio it doesn't have the luxury of using a Brand Evangelist in your social circle. Perhaps someday technology will allow everyone to watch a Superbowl ad with a different spokesperson targeting each viewer; until then, marketers have to settle for celebrities like Peyton Manning, former quarterback for the Denver Broncos.

Peyton is great. We've seen him win, we've seen him lose, and we've made an emotional connection. The degree of that connection is directly connected to the degree to which we'll make an irrational decision.

But there is a flaw in the system advertisers don't want you to know. There is no rational connection between a celebrity and a product or service (even if the celebrity has used it). This is best characterized by the fall of Tiger Woods. After his personal life was exposed, a few major brands dropped him as a spokesperson. Why? Was it because it's impossible to be a flawed human being and be a reasonable spokesman for cars or apparel? No. It's because it snapped the illusion. We really didn't know Tiger Woods. He wasn't the person we each had made him out to be in our own minds. It severed the emotional connection. No connection, no sales.

We live in an era of choice. As we continue to make choices based on someone else's experience, we enlarge a false sense of faith in ourselves. We seem to become our own best guide, and all of this pretense contributes to the collective letdown when a beloved celebrity falls from grace. It's a reminder we've set up a false sense of security. It reminds us we are not in control.

Examples of consumers being disillusioned with marketing ploys like this are why consumers took matters into their own hands, and online reviews exploded in the 2010s. Consumer reviews now exist for everything and they represent honest sentiments from Brand Evangelists and skeptics alike. They attract those buyers who believe the collective experience can be trusted to a greater degree than emotional impulse. For instance, I may see an ad that shows a regular looking guy at a restaurant surrounded by beautiful women, but if the restaurant reviews are horrible, they have the power to break that false

WHEN WE MAKE CHOICES BASED ON SOMEONE ELSE'S EXPERIENCE, WE INCREASE A FALSE SENSE OF FAITH IN OURSELVES.

emotional connection. Oprah or Dr. Oz may endorse a new book or diet, but as soon as it generates enough consumer feedback, a one-star review will overrule a celebrity endorsement. This is especially true when online consumer reviews are available at the time of purchase.

Below is a simple graph that shows how online reviews and celebrity endorsements are at the opposite end of the rational / emotional spectrum.

CONSUMER
REVIEWS

CELEB
ENDORSEMENT

RATIONAL

EMOTIONAL

The collective experience from real-life restaurant patrons, whether good or bad, becomes our new connection. Each connection changes what we know about a brand. It alters our gut feeling. The classic way of expressing this idea is through a schema, which is a graphical representation of commonly held beliefs about an organization. In the center of the radial graph is the brand, and the spokes lead to ideas or preconceived notions associated with the brand. Marketers often use this in brainstorming sessions when identifying areas that need to be addressed through public relations. For example, Nike brand managers would have identified that "sweat shops in China" became a negative brand attribute after factory conditions were reported in the news several times. The goal then is to counter that negative attribute by telling a different side of the story.

YOU ARE THE MOST POWERFUL MARKETING TOOL THE CATHOLIC CHURCH HAS.

Here is an example of what a schema might look like for the universal Catholic Church.

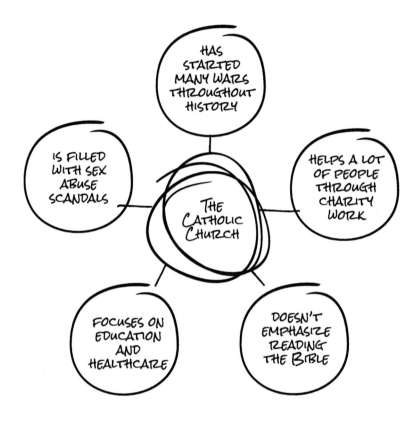

So how do we help people understand the negative or learn more about the positives? It's not through national TV ads or celebrity Catholics. The most powerful marketing tool the Catholic Church has is you. You have the ability to change the schemas regarding Catholicism to everyone you meet.

Take the example below. Notice how this person's perspective becomes centered on Bob, the Brand Evangelist, instead of the Catholic Church as it's portrayed in the news.

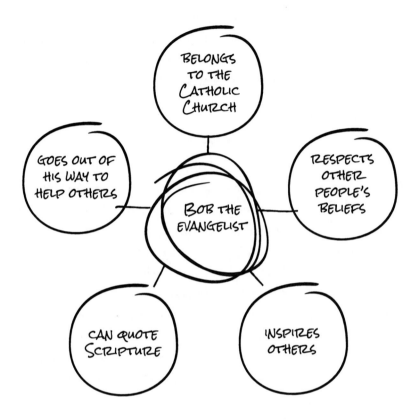

When you represent Jesus Christ and his Church, you need to understand that people are gauging their ability to have a similar experience before "trying" it themselves. People aren't looking to you to answer their toughest philosophical or theological questions; they're looking to see if you're happy, if you're fulfilled, if you're living a life of peace and wonder they want to secure for themselves. Remember, they may be experiencing fear and disappointment in their current faith system.

At the end of the day, we still make decisions based on faith. It may not seem that way, but every decision we make involves a leap of faith. We constantly seek out connections to narrow our choices.

Some of them are as strong as a personal recommendation from a Brand Evangelist and some are as superficial as the color and style of the packaging. These connections help us whittle down the number of options we have. Every time we make a decision, it adds to the illusion that we are in control.

* * *

Nobody sets out to become a dull, unhappy Christian. So how can we achieve a personal conversion that's contagious? Some of us may be struggling with disabilities, personal issues, past hurts that still throb, broken relationships, or addictions and other "isms" that seem insurmountable. In short, we aren't always happy.

A Catholic Brand Evangelist does not have to be bubbly and enthusiastic all the time. We shouldn't try to smile through clenched teeth and pretend our lives are perfect. People will be able to tell the difference between a front and the real thing almost immediately. An effective Brand Evangelists must be genuine in all circumstances, even when circumstances are bad.

As Catholics, our courage and hope during gut-wrenching trials comes from only one place—the foot of the cross. Our suffering in life becomes bearable when we put it in context of the ultimate suffering of God himself, who came down from heaven to take our punishment onto himself. One of Jesus's greatest gifts is an answer to the question "does God understand what I'm going through?"

WHAT MIGHT BE HINDERING YOUR PERSONAL CONVERSION?

***Because he himself was tested through what he suffered, he is
able to help those who are being tested. (Hebrews 2:18)***

The realization, according to St. James, that "You are a puff
of smoke that appears briefly and then disappears" (James 4:14) and
that in heaven God will "wipe every tear from their eyes, and there
shall be no more death or mourning, wailing or pain, [for] the old
order has passed away" (Revelation 21:4) should be the central fact of
our lives.

So now someone comes across our path who needs to hear our
experience. How can we be assured we'll be the Brand Evangelist God
wants us to be? How can we keep life from ruining our delivery? The
best way I know how to be a Brand Evangelist for Christ is to get out
of the way. The less I'm thinking about myself, the happier and more
aware of God's will I am. It's that simple.

A few years ago, I met a man named Doug. He is one of those
men who's short in stature but larger than life; in fact, he kind
of reminded me of Napoleon. Doug was a high-ranking officer
in the Navy stationed in Annapolis, Maryland, and was often
gone for long stretches of time. Doug was a captain and commanded some of the largest and most technologically advanced
sea craft in our naval military. It made me smile to think of him
at the helm of those huge ships. Short though he was, it was
obvious he made up for it in tenacity. I was glad he was on our
side.

One day, during our Bible study group, he shared the proce-
dure to follow when a man falls overboard. *The Navy Lookout
Training Handbook* says: "The life-buoy watch or anyone else
who sees a person fall overboard must shout as loudly as possible, without hesitation, 'Man overboard, starboard (port) side!'

This call must be repeated until the conning officer takes necessary action…" The lookout must keep his or her eyes "fixed" on the person overboard and continually point to that person. The lookout cannot glance away, even for a second, or the churning waters will obscure the person and he or she will be lost.

St. Paul tells us that we have to die to ourselves and follow Christ. If we're going to follow him we, like the lookout, cannot take our eyes off him for a second. We must keep our eyes fixed on Jesus through Scripture reading, frequent reception of holy Communion, eucharistic adoration, and prayer. A mind and heart constantly being converted to Christ, no matter life's circumstances, will always lead to a joy that extends beyond the blessings and trials of this world into the unending joys of the next.

That's the difference between a Brand Evangelist for Christ and one for a product or service. Not despite of, but because of the troubles of this world, we should shout as loudly as possible, and without hesitation, that Jesus is the answer. Jesus will never falter. He'll never be exposed on TMZ. He is the one we can always count on.

And who can forget Peter, the only man in history to walk on water? His characteristically bold attitude prompted him to challenge God to call him out on the water.

> *Peter said to him in reply, "Lord, if it is you,*
> *command me to come to you on the water."*
> *(Matthew 14:28)*

Peter walking on the water is an amazing story and one of my favorites. When Peter stayed focused on Jesus, he looked past his fears and shortcomings and moved toward the Lord. But then he did what? He took his eyes off of Jesus. Only then did he begin to sink. I often picture myself in Peter's position, and what thoughts might be going through my head.

"I'm going down!"

"I wonder if the other guys are seeing this!"

"Will the rabbi believe me?"

"I must be pretty special. Maybe I'm more special than the others."

"I'm sinking! I'm a failure. I knew I couldn't do it!"

And on and on.

This world provides us an unending litany of conflicting fears and prideful thoughts that leave us paralyzed. When we are sinking, it's because we're only thinking of ourselves. That's when the devil is most satisfied. One less Brand Evangelist for Christ to worry about.

THE BEST WAY TO BE A BRAND EVANGELIST FOR CHRIST IS TO GET OUT OF THE WAY.

CHAPTER TWO

Know Yourself

NOTHING IS MORE DIFFICULT,
FOR A PERSON OR A BRAND,
THAN TAKING AN HONEST LOOK
IN THE MIRROR.

I had spent hours in the bitter winter cold of West Virginia, surrounded by hundreds of stone relics of lives past. I was searching for a grave with my name on it. I was searching for closure. Instead, I found a headstone with a simple engraving that led to a deep, lifelong understanding of who I am. It read:

> *Husband, Father, Grandfather. You did all you could do. You loved all that you could love. In our hearts you'll always be.*

Discovering what kind of Catholic I am will be a lifelong journey, but certain life experiences have shaped my perspective so far. These experiences have created the foundation on which I have begun to build my own Catholic brand. The years leading up to that winter revelation have given me a window into the struggles of men in our culture today, especially those under the oppression of addiction. My personal Catholic brand is as unique as I am. Reflecting on my experiences, especially the difficult ones, has helped me understand how God wants to use my one-of-a-kind life to help others. Through this self-searching, I have created a better me and have become a more intentional Catholic Brand Evangelist.

The benefits of self-discovery also apply to my professional career. The most successful brands have a clear sense of what makes them different from the competition. These differentiators include the history of the company, the mission statement, and the unique value they provide. Nothing is more difficult, for a person or a brand, than taking an honest look in the mirror.

Finding Myself (A Look in the Mirror)

I was newly married, and my wife and I had just left our hometown of Columbus, Ohio, where we went to high school and college, for

South Florida. Moving to Florida was our great adventure, and we soon found a group of friends who were just as adventurous. In the middle of Florida, closer to alligator wrestlers and four wheelers than sandy beaches and universal entertainment, was Peace River. It lived up to its peaceful name—serene and perfect for canoeing. Along with a half dozen other couples, we packed everything we needed for three days into one canoe: tent, sleeping bags, food, water, clothes, chairs, and of course beer (and a bottle of Southern Comfort for when the beer ran out).

It was a shared, spiritual experience to paddle down the river for a full day searching for a spot to camp. Then everything could come out of the canoe and the shenanigans would begin! Exploring, cooking, tree climbing, swinging from limbs into the river marked the next two days. Fire, conversation, and random visits from passing cattle marked our evenings. We worked through all our provisions, especially the alcohol, so on the final day there was nothing left but a few swigs of Southern Comfort. I made sure of that. Sunday was filled with a quiet six miles with only our headaches and sunbathing alligators to keep us company. God was the furthest thing from our minds on that Sunday morning; except perhaps as a fleeting thought that it would be nice if something would take the hangover pain away and make the good feelings come back. The Southern Comfort. An oasis in the desert. Just a nip and the "spirituality" returns.

But even my marriage, sunshine, booze, and newfound friends weren't enough to make me feel complete. So I quit my job to start my own business. Now I would truly be living the purpose driven life. What could go wrong?

My timing was perfect. Web 2.0 was reawakening businesses' appetites for digital marketing on the heels of the Dot Com bubble. The Internet was becoming transactional and search engines were helping consumers connect with services and products in a way that was impossible before. Yahoo, Excite, Ask Jeeves, and a little upstart called Google were battling for position. I stepped in to offer businesses in South Florida, and later around the country, a way to compete for a coveted first-page position.

I couldn't service clients fast enough. I brought on a business partner and we quickly outgrew my home office. Approximately forty clients later, we had an office and six employees. Business was good. My marriage seemed perfect. I was woefully unprepared for the struggles ahead, in both my fledgling marriage and my new business.

Instead of planning for a rainy day, I was living like the canoe trip never ended. The purpose of life was to go from one good time to the next. But the good times always end. My most lucrative client began to withhold payment. The real estate crisis came and South Florida faced a reckoning. What I called Fun Friday turned into Thirsty Thursday, then Wacky Wednesday, Toasty Tuesday, and inevitably, Manic Monday. Happy hours began earlier and went later. Annoying absences from home led to phone dodging exasperations. Everything began to fall apart around me, and the only thing I knew to do to control my environment was, selfishly, to drink.

Selfishness, and the denial that accompanies it, was easy. If someone asked, "Why didn't you call me back?" I easily responded, "I was on an important conference call, and forgot."

> TO BE THE MAN I WANTED TO BE,
> TO LIVE A LIFE OF TRUE PURPOSE,
> I HAD TO LET GO OF ALL MY OLD IDEAS.

I did forget, not because I was too busy, but because I was drinking. Living in denial meant I could avoid criticism. I had every intention of calling them back! Over time, the denial got so thick I couldn't see the truth of my actions. It was only a matter of time before the house of cards came falling down.

As an experienced marketer, I can attest to the fact big business is behind the message your happiness is best achieved by focusing on your own wants and aspirations. I became my own economic system. By day I was selling that message of self-satisfying happiness. By night I was buying it. I was my number one priority. I became critical of those around me. I was failing to notice others' needs, and began to blame them for my failures. I began to resent my responsibilities at home and work because I felt I already worked harder than anyone. I had trouble listening to the important people in my life. When I did, I had a low appreciation of their perspective.

> WHAT IN YOUR OWN LIFE DISTRACTS YOU FROM GOD?

That selfishness came with increased drinking. That's when I lost both the office and my self-respect. For a few years, I lived in a three-bedroom cottage in hell. It was beautiful on the outside; it was one mile from the beach, held a beautiful wife and a gorgeous daughter, a successful business, a new truck, all wrapped in a white picket fence. On the inside, I was decaying.

I have never needed a new lease on life as much as I did in those last few months of my active alcoholism. To call it quits would have been merciful. It seemed like the compassionate thing to do—spare my wife, family, and business partner from having to suffer through me. The end came in an ordinary way. One sunny day, as I sat, shrouded in gloom on the back stoop of my house, I had a single thought. My way wasn't working. I needed help.

God isn't typically one for fanfare. Jesus could have turned the world inside out to prove his divinity, but instead he washed feet, he came in service. Besides, if there had been some big hullabaloo about me getting sober, it would only have fed my suspicion that the world really did revolve around me.

I was at a crossroads, and providentially, the treatment program recommended to me was called The Crossing Point. Situated in Harper's Ferry, West Virginia, it offered the solitude I needed to find a new connection with God in a safe environment. I didn't know what would happen. I couldn't see the path ahead, but I had faith in something.

I could do nothing for anyone until I completely changed myself. I'm not talking a gas station car wash kind of change either. I'm talking about a hot lava pit that melts everything down to its base elements—a complete transformation. To be the man I wanted to be, to live a life of true purpose, I had to let go of all my old ideas.

The Crossing Point introduced me to the twelve steps of recovery. In step one, I admitted I was powerless over my addiction. In step two, I came to believe a power greater than myself could free me from addiction. In step three, I made a choice to turn everything over to him. In steps four and five, I made a fearless moral inventory and confessed it to someone else. In steps six and seven, I willingly released all my selfish desires to help others. In steps eight and nine, I began to make amends to everyone I had harmed. In steps

> WITHOUT A PROPER INVENTORY OF OUR OWN MIND, OUR HEART WILL STAY CLOUDED AND CLOSED.

ten and eleven, I learned that all I had was today, and the best way to spend it was in prayer, meditation, and self-introspection. Finally in step twelve, I actively reached out to help others with no strings attached, just as I had been helped. The twelve steps transformed my life and I will be forever grateful.

I also learned later that there are many similarities between the twelve steps and my Catholic faith. For example, in St. Ignatius' spiritual exercises an examination of conscience and a good confession are both required to let go of the past and create a new future. St. John of the Cross calls it the dark night of the soul, where selfish desires are purged (in an uncomfortable way). In recovery, it's called a complete psychic change. The only thing you have to change is everything.

In my first few weeks at The Crossing Point, I was oblivious to all of this. I was consumed with myself. I was going through the toughest part of transformation, taking an honest look at myself through a written inventory. Day after day I was putting pen to paper and trudging up every item hidden in my storehouses of sin. I was reliving every stone in the wall and labeling it, not to beat myself up over it but to search for patterns of behavior. When I finished my fearless inventory I was faced with the overwhelming evidence of my past behavior. I was stuck. How could I possibly overcome a lifetime of self-seeking?

The answer came to me in that graveyard. At first I was looking for a grave with my name on it to symbolically bury my past, but the lesson God wanted me to learn was that my past shouldn't be buried and forgotten. It should be understood, forgiven, and used to heal and spread God's love. As the poem suggests, I'd done all I could do and loved all I could love with the tools I had been given. Equipped with new knowledge and divine tools, I had the ability to change the hearts of those around me.

✳ ✳ ✳

This is true with brands as well. I can't speak confidently to others as a brand marketer when there's a warehouse full of widgets I know nothing about. I can't be a witness to my Catholic faith when I have resentments I haven't acknowledged. It's the same principle. Just as any business would be severely hampered by a blind eye toward inventory, evangelization will be hampered by the evangelizer's blind eye toward his or her resentments. The concept is simple: get your own house in order before you invite people over.

The point of a spiritual inventory is not to help you magically agree with everything the Church teaches or to remove any hurt caused by personal offenses. It's the job of the Holy Spirit to guide, shape, and open our minds. Think of the Holy Spirit as the best learning and development coach of all time. Without a proper inventory of our own mind, our heart will stay clouded and closed to what the Holy Spirit wants to teach us. Without this self-knowledge, we'll struggle as Brand Evangelists. When people express their own hurts and hang-ups, they'll latch onto our hesitancy or bitterness. They'll see that we never took the time to consider ourselves in relation to the Church.

There are many different kinds of inventories. You can find them through professional counselors, twelve-step recovery groups, and even religious orders like the Jesuits. Each inventory is designed to focus on a specific area of healing and growth. For this book, we'll focus on an inventory relating to Jesus and his Catholic Church.

First, think about Jesus and the Church. Ponder any negative emotions or thoughts that come to mind. Ask yourself if these are resentments or fears. Don't overthink your responses. Just start jotting things down as they come to mind. Don't worry about offending God. He already knows, and he can take it.

Next, consider how each resentment or fear affects you person-ally. Put a checkmark in each column that applies. Finally, take a look in the mirror and honestly acknowledge your part in the resentment or fear. In the "Where Was I to Blame?" column, write out one or two character defects that sum up your role. I've added a few examples of my own to get you started.

Once you've completed the inventory sheets of negative thoughts or emotions, flip the page over and write a simple gratitude list. What

Resentment or Fear	About What? Why?	What Was Affected? (threatened or hurt)					
		Self Esteem	Personal Relations	Marital Security	Emotional Security	Sexual	
RESENTMENT	CHURCH COVERED UP SEX ABUSES				X		
RESENTMENT	MY PRIEST GROWING UP DID NOT TAKE ME OUT TO LUNCH	X	X				
FEAR	MY FAMILY WON'T GO TO HEAVEN		X		X		

positive things about Jesus and the Catholic Church are you grateful for? What good things has the Church instilled in the world and your personal life? The gratitude list is important; it grounds us in reality and balances out the negative feelings.

On the next page you'll find a list of character defects, defined by their opposite attribute. Sometimes it's helpful to contemplate the ideal to pinpoint where we fall short.

Exact Nature of Our Wrongs. Where was I?					Where was I to blame?
Dishonest	Self-Seeking	Frightened	Ungrateful	Resentful	
		X		X	
			X		
		X			

CHARACTER DEFECTS	CHARACTER ASSETS
conceited, self-important, vain	humble, modest
controlling	let go, especially of other's lives
critical	non-judgmental, praising, tolerant,
dishonest	honest
envying	empathetic, generous, admiring
false pride	modest, humble
fantasizing, unrealistic	practical, realistic
fearful	confident, courageous
gluttonous, excessive	moderate
gossiping	closed-mouth, kind, praising
greedy	moderate, generous, sharing
impatient	patient
impulsive, reckless	consistent, considered actions
intolerant	tolerant, understanding, patient
jealous	trusting, generous, admiring
judgmental	broadminded, tolerant
justifying (own actions)	honest, frank, candid
lustful	healthy sexuality
manipulative	candid, honest, non-controlling
over sensitive	emotionally stable
perfectionist	realistic goals
procrastinates	disciplined, acts promptly
rationalizing	candid, honest
resentful	forgiving
self-pity	grateful, realistic, accepting
self-seeking	selfless, concerned for others
selfish	altruistic, concerned with others
ungrateful	thankful, grateful

Remember, as we evangelize the first step is connecting with people on an emotional level. We aren't expected to have all the answers. Answer what you can. Research things you don't know or direct people to a trusted online resource or parish priest. Just don't make something up.

If you're living a life of purpose and are filled with the Holy Spirit, it will be evident, and others will desire that kind of life. When your experience includes a mature personal assessment of all your hang-ups about the Church past to present, they'll see a true Brand Evangelist. Your hang-ups most likely won't be the same as those you encounter. But that's OK. Those searching for meaning want to meet someone who has moved through seemingly insurmountable fears and resentments to find peace in the faith. The fruits of your personal honesty will give others the courage to open themselves up to the Holy Spirit.

For a full list and printable inventory sheets,
visit www YouAreTheCatholicBrand.com

Creating a Personal Mission Statement

Another great thing about carefully examining your past is that it gives you the ability to understand your present and provides a guide for the future. Every great brand has a clear sense of its past and its core mission.

> Take Starbucks for example, one of the best known brands in the world. When you read their mission statement, notice how you get a sense of their heritage, their daily focus, and their future goals in one sentence. *Our mission: To inspire and nurture the human spirit—one person, one cup, and one neighborhood at a time.*
>
> Now think about a Starbucks near you. Individualized service—every cup they brew is unique. Accomplished baristas anticipate the needs of repeat customers. The business becomes part of the neighborhood. Starbucks is successful, in part, because each shop becomes a destination. They are places people go to relax or talk with a friend, and leave feeling inspired.

Mission statements help us begin the journey of preparedness. Forming a personal mission statement is an important tool for internalizing your core beliefs and attitudes. Many brands only use their mission statement for internal training and motivation. That's what your personal mission statement should do: orient you toward a set of goals and principles that help guide your faith.

A mission statement can be created only when you know who you are and where you want to go. The only way to know who you are is to spend more time discovering who God created you to be. St. Paul makes it clear that every one of us has unique gifts given by the Holy

Spirit. The combination and manifestation of these gifts in your life is uniquely yours. No one else can fulfill your role in the world.

> "There are different kinds of spiritual gifts but the same Spirit; there are different forms of service but the same Lord; there are different workings but the same God who produces all of them in everyone. To each individual the manifestation of the Spirit is given for some benefit. To one is given through the Spirit the expression of wisdom; to another the expression of knowledge according to the same Spirit; to another faith by the same Spirit; to another gifts of healing by the one Spirit; to another mighty deeds; to another prophecy; to another discernment of spirits; to another varieties of tongues; to another interpretation of tongues. But one and the same Spirit produces all of these, distributing them individually to each person as he wishes." (1 Corinthians 12:4–11)

One of the best ways to find out your spiritual gifts is to ask someone, especially someone close to you. They will have insights into the ways you are gifted that you may not recognize. There are also several fantastic spiritual gift inventory quizzes online that will walk you through a series of questions and then give you some possible recommendations.

YOUR PERSONAL MISSION STATEMENT SHOULD ORIENT YOU TOWARD THE GOALS THAT HELP GUIDE YOUR FAITH.

First, and foremost, God loves you beyond your imagination. That is the central fact you need to know about yourself when building a spiritual mission statement. Through your baptism and faith in Christ, God promises you peace in this life and immeasurable riches in the next. He has the same longing for every person in your family, at your office, along the highways, in media, and everywhere else. God's love for all of humanity is inexplicable. God's love is freely given and must be freely accepted. So take it!

When crafting your mission statement, it's important to keep a few principles in mind. First, narrow your areas of focus to two or three things. It can be daunting when you try to list all of your interests. Second, stress the things that matter most to you. Finally, keep your mission statement short. If you get too carried away, you won't remember it.

Taking everything you've just learned about yourself into account, use the following formula to create a spiritual mission statement for yourself. Start by filling in the blanks below. My answers are in parentheses as an example.

God loves me.

1. I grew up _____.
   (CATHOLIC)

2. My faith became my own when I _____.
   (STRUGGLED WITH ALCOHOLISM)

3. Some doubts I have are _____.
   (THAT I CAN SUPPORT MY FAMILY AS AN AUTHOR)

4. Some fears I have are _____.
   (I WILL NOT BE ABLE TO STAY SOBER)

5. Some resentments I have are _____.
   (GOD HASN'T CURED ME OF ADDICTION)

6. Some things I currently do to move past these doubts, fears, and
   resentments are _____.
   (DAILY SCRIPTURE READING, FAMILY ROSARY, HANGING
   OUT WITH MEN OF FAITH.)

7. My spiritual talents include _____.
   (EVANGELIZATION)

8. I have a soft spot for _____.
   (MEN WHO STRUGGLE WITH ADDICTION)

9. I have a hard time understanding or relating to _____.
   (MIDDLE SCHOOLERS AND TEENAGERS)

10. I have the most influence with _____.
    (MEN IN MY CHURCH)

11. I have the least influence with _____.
    (NEIGHBORS)

12. _____ is what I want the most
    from my Catholic faith. (PEACE AND SERENITY)

God loves me.

Now take your answers and fill in the sample personal mission statement below.

To _____ (7) is my primary objective. I

concentrate my efforts on _____ (10)

and _____ (8). But I realize I need to

expand my efforts with _____ (9) and

_____ (11).

I move past my fears and gain strength through

_____ (6). When given

the opportunity, I will evangelize by relating how I grew up

_____ (1) and was fully converted

when _____ (2).

Remembering, each day, that God loves me, I will seek his will in order

to achieve _____ (12).

DID YOU CREATE
YOUR PERSONAL
MISSION STATEMENT?

Here is my personal mission statement using the formula above.

TO EVANGELIZE IS MY PRIMARY OBJECTIVE.
I CONCENTRATE MY EFFORTS ON MEN IN MY
CHURCH AND THOSE STRUGGLING WITH ADDICTION.
BUT I REALIZE I NEED TO EXPAND MY EFFORTS
WITH MIDDLE SCHOOLERS, TEENAGERS, AND
NEIGHBORS.

I MOVE PAST MY FEARS AND GAIN STRENGTH
THROUGH DAILY SCRIPTURE READING AND
HANGING OUT WITH MEN OF FAITH. WHEN GIVEN THE
OPPORTUNITY, I WILL EVANGELIZE BY RELATING
HOW I GREW UP CATHOLIC AND WAS FULLY
CONVERTED WHEN I STRUGGLED WITH ALCOHOLISM.

REMEMBERING, EACH DAY, THAT GOD LOVES ME, I
WILL SEEK HIS WILL IN ORDER TO ACHIEVE PEACE AND
SERENITY.

Now that you have created a solid mission statement, it's time to put it in action. The best way to do that is to learn more about your personal "customers."

Chapter Three

Know Your Customers

WE CAN'T COMMUNICATE
EFFECTIVELY UNTIL WE KNOW WHO
WE'RE TALKING TO.

After I accepted a position as the director of marketing for a national apartment building and management company, I received a heavy packet in the mail. At first I thought it might be company swag, maybe even a new iPad. Disappointingly, it was a six-inch-thick stack of paper. I couldn't imagine how all this paper related to my new job. I worried it contained all the previous marketing efforts to show me the way it had always been done. I held my breath. What I found in that mound of papers was a gold mine. The packet was filled with customer data.

Like most companies that establish a successful brand, this one had made a serious investment in the collection and analysis of customer data. In fact, many companies will spend more on the customer research than they will on the subsequent brand marketing. No one can communicate effectively until he or she knows who they're talking to. And not just their name, age, and gender. You also have to know your customer's preferences. Real estate preferences include price versus location, convenience versus amenities, and luxury versus value. As you get to know someone's preferences, you can tweak your delivery to fit them. This means more than just targeting someone for a sale. It shows that you took the time to get to know them and meet them where they are.

There are two ways companies understand audience preferences on a mass scale. The first is through mountains of data such as the census or university studies. News agencies use these all the time—a provocative headline grabs attention and generates comments. The article usually starts something like, "47% of Americans think…" When you read a statistic like that, your skeptical hackles should raise. A poll is only as reliable as the sampling, collection method, and market researcher who compiled it. Those details are usually buried in the article, if they're mentioned at all.

The second way to understand audience preferences is by listening to or observing small groups of people interact with a product or service. The old Life cereal commercial exemplifies this method, when the older brothers push the bowl to little Mikey and Mikey's eyes light up as soon as he takes a bite. A survey about whether Mikey did or didn't like the cereal could never compare to observing the actual experience he had and the "fact" that Mikey never likes anything but loved that cereal.

> THERE'S A DIFFERENCE BETWEEN OBSERVING AND JUST COLLECTING DATA.

Listening to customer comments can't be boiled down to a chart. Findings from listening and observing are the most difficult to collect and near impossible to compile, yet they remain the most valuable when it comes to predicting how people will respond to new things.

Online product reviews are a unique blend of both strategies. When you're looking for your next vacation getaway, the hotel ratings help you compare options. The experiences of others stated in those reviews become invaluable to us as we make a decision.

My cousin Tommy is a pilot for a big passenger airline and an online review freak. He has perfected the art of analyzing reviews for everything from hotels to restaurants to public restrooms because he travels so frequently. Tommy often takes the lead when planning where our family will dine during the annual Kilmurry family vacation. His proficiency is amazing. Tommy takes a quick survey for which types of food family members are in the mood for and the price range people are willing to spend. Five minutes later he's leading us to a restaurant we otherwise never would have tried.

There's also a difference between observing and just collecting data.

Paul and Jamie are a couple who have been through a lot both together and as individuals. Paul struggled with depression and one night drove his car into a wall in a suicide attempt. The doctors worked hard to put his body back together and save his life. He now has scars and metal plates everywhere, and heart issues for the rest of his life. During his recovery, he became addicted to pain pills. Then came seizures. He still struggles to keep a job and to stay sober. Jamie was also in recovery from addiction to pills. She has a small child from a previous, abusive relationship. She eventually joined a twelve-step group and made progress toward healing.

When Paul and Jamie started dating, they decided it was best to give it a full "trial run" before getting married. During the next few years it seemed to go from bad to worse. Paul's seizures increased in frequency and he relapsed into using pain medication. Jamie became pregnant with their first child together. The pregnancy and the birth were extremely hard on Jamie. She spent most of it on bed rest and in constant pain. Their beautiful baby girl was born with problems of her own, which demanded the last ounces of energy from Paul. Paul loved his family despite all their hardships, and he tried to care for them the best he could.

Paul's faith in God deepened and he began to notice God's presence in his life. For Paul, God had no name. Jamie, on the other hand, harbored deep resentments against the Christian God because of a trauma in her past. One night Shannon and I invited them to join us for dinner. Because our children were small, we began to feel trapped at home. Truthfully, the invite seemed more for us than for them.

When Paul and Jamie showed up my children immediately bolted outside to greet them before they stepped out of the car.

Our children didn't care who it was in the car or what problems they experienced—they were new friends! Conversation flowed easily and we shared some laughs. We commiserated about the chaos children cause. I prayed over the meal with the adults. My six-year-old daughter led the children in prayer. We allowed the kids to watch a Disney movie after dinner while the adults enjoyed a relaxing cup of coffee.

That was it. However, a few weeks later Paul surprised me with a call and told me how much our time and friendship that evening meant to them. He also related that they had decided to move up their plans to marry. A few months before the wedding, he asked me to be a groomsman.

Looking back, I can see how I unknowingly tailored "my message" to fit the audience. I had all the quantitative and qualitative data I needed going into the meeting. I knew both Paul's and Jamie's background and where they stood on issues of God and marriage. I instinctively knew that I would serve them best by modeling a positive example of faith in Christ and marital commitment. By doing so, we were able to alter their schema that night. Now, when they thought of marriage and Christianity, it wasn't just societal fears and personal tragedies.

> **All Catholics should know trends in the Catholic Church at all levels.**

This new insight was possible because my family provided Paul and Jamie with an experience. They knew I was a Christian and they knew I was married, but it was their shared personal experience of a married Christian with his family that made the difference. Creating a culture of encounter is the heart of Pope Francis's message. It could also be framed as a "culture of experience." But in order to know what experiences are best for whom, we have to get to know our neighbors.

There is a trove of data regarding the stresses and pressures facing our society at large. This data lays the groundwork from which we, as Catholic Brand Evangelists, might begin our work. We have all heard the statistic that half of all first marriages end in divorce. (But did you know that percentage is significantly lower when it comes to couples that state their faith is the most important thing in their marriage?)

This and many other societal trends in modern America are having a profound impact on our culture. None of us are immune. We are all walking around with some sort of wound. We are all in search of healing. As Christians, it just so happens that we have the spiritual solution.

Add to victims of divorce those who have lost their faith in Christ or those who feel disillusioned with his Church. All Catholics should know trends in the Catholic Church at all levels–internationally, nationally, and in their diocese. And not just attendances and fiscal health. Knowing more data about our Church will help us all engage more intentionally.

There are many interesting facts about the Catholic Church in the United States, such as:

- If current trends continue, deacons will outnumber priests by 2025.
- The new normal is attending Mass once a month, not weekly.
- The fastest growing demographic is Hispanic, not white or African American.
- More than ever, people parish shop, often traveling past closer churches to attend the one they prefer.

(source: http://www.cara1964.org/staff/webpages/steadychanges.pdf)

Now you're armed with a general sense of some environmental factors that may be affecting the people you encounter. But be careful, there is no faster way to alienate someone than to make a correlation between their personal experiences and choices and a broader cultural trend. That's one of the reasons brands hold on to their customer research like Coke guards its secret recipe. Imagine how off putting it would be for a monthly Mass attender to be referred to as the new normal statistic. Trends are important for us to know, but they are just that. People aren't stats, and while statistics are useful we still need to treat people like individuals.

None of this quantitative data really matters until you've gathered some qualitative data. Get to know each person you encounter a little better. You will be amazed at what you receive when you keep your heart open. Sometimes it's opportunities for expressing compassion, acts of service, or just listening with a smile. Other times the tables turn and we receive inspiration through the sharing of wisdom or a powerful witness to the life-altering effects of the Good News. The great thing about gathering qualitative data is it's easy to do. The only thing standing in our way is usually our own fear, fear of rejection, being judged, insulting someone, making them feel uncomfortable, and on and on. These fears can prevent us from becoming effective Catholic Brand Evangelists.

> FOCUS ON WHO, WHAT, WHEN, AND WHERE QUESTIONS. AVOID QUESTIONS WITH QUICK YES OR NO ANSWERS.

When I think of my own work as a Catholic Brand Evangelist, I think of my friend Edward, a southern Christian who leaves a wake of God's will in his path.

One Tuesday evening I accompanied Edward to a homeless shelter in one of the most poverty-stricken areas of Baltimore, Maryland. Edward had asked me to give my witness during the worship service and he used the drive as a chance to learn more about me. I felt privileged that he was taking an interest in me.

On the way, we stopped at a gas station. I stepped out with Edward to continue our conversation when a man in an oversized jacket and pants with an overgrown beard came up and asked us if we had any spare change. Before I could even decide how I was going to respond, Edward started talking.

"I don't give out money but let me ask you friend, do you know Jesus Christ?"

That about did it for me. The forwardness of Edward's response made me completely uncomfortable. I think I actually started to melt. But I was surprised by the man's response.

"I know the Lord," he replied confidently.

"That's wonderful," Edward continued. "You said you had a family. Are they nearby?"

The conversation kept going for a few more minutes. Our new friend told us how he was sleeping on someone's couch while he tried to find a place for his wife and kids. Edward offered to bring some food to his family and to give him a ride to the homeless shelter. Despite the man's rejection of Edward's offer, he asked one final question.

"Is there anything I can do for you?"

"Pray for me and my family," requested the homeless man.

Edward asked for each family member's name and then the man moved on to other potential givers. The whole encounter was over before the gas stopped pumping, but Edward and his family prayed for that man and his family for weeks. Edward even asked our Bible study group to do the same. It was a much greater gift than a few dollars—not just for that man but for me as well.

Edward is a model for effective Christian Brand Evangelists, but for different reasons than you may think. What the story of Edward teaches us is **how to ask questions**. The man is a qualitative data gathering machine. I have often thought back to that experience as I merged my professional training as a brand marketer with my personal vocations. Whether it was in the car ride with me, at the gas station with the homeless man, or when we got to the shelter, Edward expressed interest in the personal challenges of each person he met.

A classic corporate example of this is the **Ritz Carlton** brand. They are famous for asking questions that go beyond the standard or expected. A Ritz employee may ask you if you like dark or milk chocolate, whether you prefer firm or soft pillows, or if you enjoy sunrises or sunsets more. They do a fantastic job remembering each of your personal preferences using a sophisticated database. When you next stay at a Ritz your room will have your favorite chocolate, pillow, and view. Their attention to detail creates an immediate emotional connection.

Edward doesn't have the sophisticated computer database of the Ritz, but he does possess a mighty fine memory. When he asks questions he opens himself up to the guidance of the Holy Spirit. His message could be evangelistic, encouraging, challenging, catechetical, compassionate, or a hundred other things. Edward opens himself so people can have an experience of their own.

When gathering information yourself, focus your questions on who, what, when, and where. Questions like this force people to think before answering. Maybe people slide through life without thinking about their relationship with God. When they ponder the divine, it allows the Holy Spirit to work. Avoid asking yes/no questions because we can get conditioned to answer those without thinking. As for "why" questions, I recommend caution. Questions such as "why do you only go to Church once a month?" can make people defensive and more likely to shut off quickly. "Why" questions are typically very personal, perhaps best left for conversations after you've really gotten to know your friend.

I also recommend that you share your own personal experiences with your friend when asking questions. This helps build relationships, can make you both more comfortable, and gives your friend a chance to open up. Be honest. Don't try to make yourself into something you are not. Our own struggles can often be a great way to connect with others.

WHO IS THE "EDWARD" IN YOUR LIFE?

Here are some examples of questions you can ask to get a conversation started:

Instead of: "I haven't seen you in a while. Do you only go to church once a month?"

Ask: "Boy, I didn't hear much of the homily this morning because my kids were acting up. What did you get from it?"

Instead of: "Having a good day?"

Ask: "There must be something in the air, my kids were all behaving today! How was it getting the whole family to Mass this morning?"

Instead of: "Did you like the Mass this morning?"

Ask: "What was your favorite part of Mass this morning?"

Instead of: "Are you interested in attending the men's/women's group?"

Ask: "The men's/women's group has helped me feel at home here at the parish. What would you think about joining me this week?"

I first put this to the test on a trip home to see my family. I was amazed at how little I actually knew about the state of my family's faith life, and it cemented my desire to put the art of asking probing questions into ongoing practice with everyone God puts in my path.

My father has been getting older. I know he's always been aging, but it seemed like the rate of his oldness had really increased. For years, I would travel home for holidays and he would look like his same old self. But a visit home to the Washington, D.C., area one year really brought out the old in him. It shouldn't have, but it came as a shock to me—my dad was really old! It occurred to me that I was probably missing some of his last good years. Dad, as I had known him, was limited.

One night, I got an email alert for a discounted round trip ticket between Baltimore and Columbus. Hours later, I had a flight booked for the coming weekend to fly out Saturday and return Sunday morning. The deal gave me a limited window, so I'd have to insert myself into whatever plans my dad and brother already had.

Little did I know, God Almighty had already set our schedule, and I was just along for the ride. Sometimes traveling can be very difficult and taxing, but this trip was a breeze. Everyone I encountered was pleasant and in good spirits. The lines were short and the weather provided a smooth flight. We even caught a tailwind and arrived early.

My pops was already in the cell phone lot when my plane touched down. It felt great to hop into his worn-out Ford Explorer. For some reason, he didn't appear as old as the last time. (Perhaps that's what happens when a dad and son get together unexpectedly for an appointment from God.)

It wasn't long before I found out what was on the docket for the day. We were first on our way to my brother Mike's house for lunch and then tagging along to watch my niece compete in an intramural basketball game. Afterwards we would regroup at Mike's and then head over to Our Lady of Perpetual Help, where I grew up, for Saturday Mass with the whole family. Finally, we would ditch the kids and have an adult dinner at Outback Steakhouse. Overall, a fantastic day of family bonding. I had no idea lives would be changed through the asking of some simple questions.

On the drive home from the basketball game, it was just my dad, my brother, and me. Three Kilmurry men caught up on God's good flow.

"How was your Easter?" I asked, avoiding the yes/no variation "did you have a good Easter?"

"I was hoping to make it to confession before Easter," my brother seemed to say offhand. "But I never had the chance to go."

Bam! Nothing could have prepared me for that answer. That was all God.

It was a shocking and startling statement because my family didn't talk about things as personal as confession, and from my brother it was particularly out of character. It must have been brewing for some time and the Holy Spirit seized the moment. Either way, a door had been opened. Just like my willingness to be open to God's plan had given him permission to arrange the menu, so too was my brother's admission a way of handing over his will to God.

"Yeah. I think the rule is at least once a year during Lent," I said in my most cavalier voice.

"What kept you from going this Lent?" I asked, pivoting to another W question.

"They only offer confession for 45 minutes on Saturday before Mass," Mike said. "There's always something going on Saturdays at 4."

"Well, what time is it? Why don't we go today?" There. I said it. Once you say something like that, there's no going back.

"It's only three o'clock," Mike said. "We'd have to go home first."

"Or we could just go now," I said. "Be the first in line. You know, spend some time in prayer before." God please, I thought, don't let this opportunity slide away!

"Well, what about Dad?" Mike seemed to plead. "We'd have to drop him all the way at his house."

"Hey Dad," I said, throwing my voice to the back seat

searching for my next probing question. "What do you think about going to confession today?"

"When?" He yelled back.

"Right now," I replied.

"OK. I'll go," he agreed matter-of-factly. His willingness had to be God at work.

There was a moment of silence. It was thick and breath catching.

"Let me call my wife," Mike mumbled, most likely hoping for one last chance to be rescued. He pulled out his phone and tapped a few commands.

"Hey honey," he spoke lightly into the phone. "We were thinking of stopping at church and going to confession at four. Did I need to be home for anything?"

Mike didn't know he was caught up in a spiritual current and there was no answer other than "no honey" that could have come from the other end. He put the phone down and paused for a moment.

"I hope it's not Father _____," Mike said grandiosely. "I won't ever be able to show my face again."

"You better tell him to get comfortable," wheezed Dad breaking the tension.

We laughed. All three of us, with excitement, nerves, and dread.

The remainder of the ride was jovial. When we pulled up to the church, it was a wasteland. The parking lot appeared so lifeless you would have thought we'd survived the zombie apocalypse. We exited the car and shuffled to the door.

Despite our misgivings about the barrenness of the parking lot, the inside of the church was bright and inviting. The incense and stained glass sunlight provided a familiar backdrop.

There was an underground lake sense of quiet and still. This was truly a place where our Lord resided. We had been led here to face him, admit our faults, and ask for forgiveness. It's no small thing to do. I had asked for forgiveness in the quiet of my mind, but now we were here to voice it aloud in front of God and a witness. That sure makes it harder. But God isn't looking for easy. He's looking for conversions. Maybe that's why Jesus chose men to administer God's power of forgiveness when he said to them at Pentecost, "whose sins you forgive are forgiven them, and whose sins you retain are retained" (John 20:23).

We blessed ourselves with holy water as we entered and sat down in a row of chairs next to the confessional. There we were, the three Kilmurry men in line for confession. It was wildly out of the ordinary, but something about it felt right and true. Families should go to confession together. There is some kind of bonding that happens. I've never felt anything similar.

I pulled out my smartphone and a quick search led me to an examination of conscience based on the Ten Commandments. As I reviewed the list, my heart sank. I had done everything on that list, and more. I passed it over to Mike and saw an expression that mirrored my inside. The moment had become very real. Mike and I were both sweating.

Mike couldn't take it anymore, "I'm going first."

I was sitting closest to the confessional, but that didn't matter to Mike. The firefighter took over. There was a red-hot blaze inside that room and he would be the first man in. If the fire consumed him, if hell opened up and swallowed him whole, if lightning struck him dead on his knees, at least his dad and brother would have a chance to survive. A human peace offering for the failings of the family.

Mike handed my phone to Dad and the moment he read

"examination of conscience" he promptly handed it back to Mike, with a snicker that said "Oh, hell no."

We both giggled and the situation lost some of its grandiosity. We were three men again, sitting on chairs, waiting for the priest to arrive. Mike let out a noticeable sigh of relief when the priest arrived. It was a visiting priest. What luck!

Firefighter Mike jumped up. If these were his last moments in human form, then he would face them like a man. Dad didn't seem to notice. In fact, he might have been sleeping. I settled in for the duration. I shifted in my seat. It was going to be a long wait. Just a few short minutes later, Mike emerged. I was shocked. He had been in there for less than five minutes. In fact, it was more like three. Mike had a Cheshire grin, ear to ear.

My time had arrived. I would tell you what happened next, really I would, but I'm not allowed. What happens in the confessional stays in the confessional. But when the final blessing was said, and my sins were forgiven, that's exactly how I felt. Pristinely clean.

"I've never felt better," said Mike when I met him in the vestibule. "You know, it's been years since I've been to confession. Man that was so easy!"

I was elated. My own sense of relief and surprise at hearing how long Mike had been away from the sacrament of reconciliation combined with an overwhelming feeling that everything was right with the world. The three of us became closer that day than we had ever been before.

One week later, back in Baltimore, I was trimming my bushes when I received a call from my mother.

"Hey Mom," I panted.

"Hello son," came her familiar, cheery voice. "I just wanted to call you and tell you what you started."

"Oh yeah?" I said clueless. I was half paying attention as I picked up debris.

"Your brother just took all three of his daughters to confession for the first time as a family," she said. "We often never know how our actions affect other people, so I thought I'd let you know."

I stopped in mid stoop and slowly stood up. I lifted my eyes beyond the horizon as I took in the meaning of her words. All that from one simple question, "How was your Easter?" I hadn't meant to gather qualitative data that day. I hadn't meant to become a Brand Evangelist for the sacrament of reconciliation, but by allowing the Holy Spirit to guide that normal interaction, something powerful happened.

✖✖✖

So how exactly do we go about collecting this data on our own?

Don't be afraid to write stuff down. In the men's adult faith formation group I lead we have upwards of twenty men attend every week. I want to make good connections with each person, but it's all I can do to remember names, let alone the names of the men's wives and children. Over time, I've gotten to know these men on a more personal level through one-on-one conversations.

To write their important information in a notebook may sound creepy, but we take notes in just about every other situation in life. Whether in class, at a conference, or in a business meeting, we would look flippant if we didn't at least have a notebook or laptop open and ready. You don't have to jot down details during the actual conversation, but that evening or the next day make your notes. It's important for me to remember who has a child with a disability, who is going through a painful divorce, and dozens of other important details about what is weighing them down or lifting them up. I know I can't do that well if I don't write it down.

Try it. The next time you're headed to your group, to church, to a sports activity, and so forth, quickly review the list in the same way you would review notes prior to your next meeting. You'll not only walk in feeling confident and prepared, you'll be ready to personalize your message. An added benefit to maintaining this notebook is that it's an easy transition to a book of intentions. How often do we say, "I'll pray for you" in a conversation with friends and coworkers? How often do we remember to pray for them? Now, you'll have an easy to use repository of prayer intentions. My family places this book on our kitchen table during dinner and prays for the conversion and comfort of all those listed as well as for specific interventions related to surgeries, recoveries, struggling marriages, and so on. The book can be as organized or as simple as you'd like. Whatever form it takes, you'll end up with a book worth its weight in gold and a better understanding of why brands invest so much in their customer profiles.

What does this look like in daily practice? Do you have to walk around asking the preferences of everyone you meet? Not really, it's more about being intentional in our already set up God appointments. We need to keep our eyes and ears open during daily interactions. We need to be open to the Holy Spirit working in others. Only then do we have an opportunity to participate in his plan. Sometimes being open to the Holy Spirit and providing meaningful encounters is hardest with those closest to us. We don't need notes on them, but that familiarity can also breed complacency.

> ALL CATHOLICS SHOULD KNOW TRENDS IN THE CATHOLIC CHURCH AT ALL LEVELS.

Questions can be very powerful. Our minds are trained from years of schooling to automatically answer the question even if we don't want to. "What have you done for your marriage today?" That was the question the USCCB asked married couples as part of their For Your Marriage campaign. It was accompanied by TV spots, billboards, and a content-rich website to help marriages.

"What have you done for your marriage today?" was perfect. First, it made people think about their marriage, which is half the battle. But it also made them think about what they've done. It put the focus on efforts outside of any met or unmet expectations of their spouse. It put the query into a daily context, which is the true secret of a successful marriage.

Many brands develop that "one question" that gets to the heart of what their customers want. I have also found this to be useful in developing a personal Catholic brand. While asking the same question is certainly not always practical, when appropriate, the answers give us ways to compare and understand where different people may be struggling or improving in the same ways. When developing your own question, think about one that gets to the heart of the matter when it comes to asking about faith. It's important that the question cuts through all the worldly trappings and encourages an honest response.

Below is my question:

"HOW IS YOUR SPIRITUAL CONDITION?"

Let's break down the components—which will help you develop your own.

"How." I use "how" instead of "what." It may seem more appropriate to ask "what," but that answer usually becomes a laundry list of activities (such as, I pray every morning, I go to adoration Friday night, and so on). While activities are usually the by-product of a healthy spirituality, they are not the cause of one. I've asked this question enough to know that people can be going through the motions while feeling totally disconnected.

As human beings, our spiritual condition changes daily because we are in a relationship with God, just like a spouse, family member, or friend. Each day we have to say yes to Christ. Some days we say it more enthusiastically than others. Some days we say nothing at all.

Knowing where someone stands is not a one-time survey. Your book of friends should not be the parish directory. Asking this question will allow you to understand how people important to you have changed over time. It's how the strongest emotional connections are made.

"Your." Your is another important word. We often find ourselves asking, "How is the family?" It is a heartfelt question, but never goes below the surface. This question will return a litany of activities or stresses, but it doesn't help you understand the active connections, fears, or misunderstandings of the person right in front of you. Spiritual lives are nurtured and strengthened at the group level but it's entirely possible to be surrounded by and participating in Church activities and feel completely disconnected from God. As St. Paul says, "work out your salvation with fear and trembling" (Philippians 2:12).

"Spiritual." General spirituality can be a nonthreatening conversation starter, especially if someone has had a bad experience with Catholics or the Church. From the weekly Mass attender to the completely unchurched, every one has a sense of their own spirituality.

"Condition." Another good word for our culture. "What's the condition of your car?" "What's the condition of your 401k?" Most people can immediately tell you the condition of the things that mean the most to them. Whether it's their body, car, golf clubs, lawn, living room, child's social, athletic, or academic standing, career, or a number of other things, we keep good track in our minds. Most often a response wouldn't require much thought. In fact, even while writing this I can tell you that two of my golf clubs need new grips, my golf shoes need new spikes—and I'm a poor golfer!

However, many people have no idea about the condition of their spirituality. Often this question will make someone consider it for the first time, outside of the stuff they do. That's when I have gotten true data—the kind that has helped me effectively communicate the Catholic Christian brand.

Now you are armed with an understanding of the environment we all live in, details of the lives being lived around you in your book of friends, and guidance on ways to ask effective questions—including one that is personal to you. Now all you need is a willingness to be open to the Holy Spirit and you're ready to personalize your message.

Chapter
Four

Personalize
Your Message

WE ARE ALWAYS EVANGELIZING
OTHERS WITH EVERY ACTION,
INACTION, AND WORD.

Moo. That was the only word on a billboard near my hometown of Grove City, Ohio. It captured my attention, and I imagine, the attention of everyone else who drove down that sleepy road toward the United Dairy Farmer's quick stop. I was a new driver, curious about what I was seeing on the road. I'm sure I'd been impacted by marketing messages before, but the Moo billboard made me aware of their effects. A few weeks later the billboard read "Moo-lah, play the Ohio Lottery." Genius. I was hooked—not on playing the lotto, but on the ways marketing messages can disrupt our lives or make us think.

I have spent the last twenty years trying to convince you to choose a particular life insurance provider or real estate agent or dozens of other products and services over others. More often than not, I have been successful. I admit that sometimes this required considerable effort pulling emotional strings. One constant I have observed and tracked with statistics galore, is the willingness of consumers to listen. When something activates a desire or need we become more open to that idea. We may only have a few seconds to make an impression, but people are rarely closed to an idea entirely. In my experience, people do change their minds. The key is having a fresh message.

The Good News of Jesus Christ has been proclaimed for over two thousand years in nearly every language and country in the world. Our country has been predominantly Christian from its birth. Is it possible to present the Gospel in new, attention-grabbing ways today? Most definitely, yes!

More now than ever we need to be creative. Many in our country are rejecting organized religion in favor of a self-governed spirituality that has no connection to Jesus Christ. The prevailing feeling is one of freedom—finally shedding the "shackles" of religion. The Internet and social media connect us in new and exciting ways, but can also be loudspeakers for those with no sense of the sacred. I have seen complex theological concepts dumbed-down into simple dismissive graphics and anonymous statements. To present the Gospel in creative ways that will capture the hearts of our culture today, we need to be cognizant of the right opportunities and aware that we are always evangelizing others with every action, inaction, and word. Each day becomes a chance to evangelize. When we evangelize, we don't always get to be the clerk at the store ringing up the final sale. The measure of how well we're evangelizing isn't how many people we have brought into full communion with the Church. There will be times people come to us ready to make the final journey home, but even then, there were others before us who contributed to their conversion.

MORE NOW THAN EVER WE NEED TO BE CREATIVE.

In the marketing world, we call this a conversion funnel. The funnel represents the process involved in generating new business. The length of time it takes to move a customer through the funnel is different for every industry, but the funnel is always the same. For example, the purchase process takes much longer for automobiles or real estate than it does for shoes or cleaning products. The best brands realize that people need to be reconverted, even after making a purchase, so they continue to find new and creative ways to entice people back into the funnel.

The standard marketing funnel looks like this:

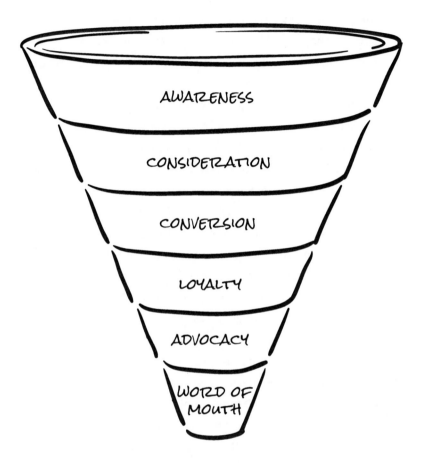

First we become aware of a product or service. This could be through an advertisement or a personal referral. That awareness leads us to consider whether the product or service fills a need. If not, we move on. If yes, we take action by purchasing, joining, subscribing, and so on. If the product or service meets or exceeds our expectations, we become loyal to that brand over the competition. That loyalty will spur us to learn more about the product or service and eventually tell others about it.

The door-to-door salesman of yesteryear represented a time companies only focused on the consideration and conversion sections of the conversion funnel. The salesperson would arrive at your home and say, "I have a selection of household cleaners for your consideration." You would listen and then either buy or not. Even when the concept of advertising grew, its sole purpose was to create awareness. The rest was up to the salesperson. It reminds me of the classic television and newspaper ads touting the price, features, and benefits of a product. The ad was meant to create awareness of the product and entice customers to visit the local store where a salesperson would help them decide if and which product to purchase. Today we can't always count on walking into a store and finding someone with the knowledge to help us make a decision. Companies rely more on brand and less on salespeople to move customers from awareness to word of mouth. This is accomplished through messaging, celebrity endorsements, promotions, websites, email campaigns, guarantees and return policies, online reviews, and on and on. Today's customers often move through the funnel without ever interacting with a human being.

The opposite is true with our Catholic brand. The faith has always been transmitted from one person to another. The Church plays a significant role in anchoring the faith, but it's the people in each age that make up the Church. The faith has been transmitted through Scripture, Tradition, the writings of contemporary or early Church fathers, and through personal encounters with other Christians. Have you ever wondered why God chose to reveal the most important truths in human history through people? He could easily have cast the writings on indestructible material in a language that would enable every person who would ever live to read them with ease. We might never fully understand this mystery, but it makes one thing clear—even the transmission of the divine is meant to be a human experience on earth.

Another stark difference between modern-day branding and the transmission of faith is that moving through the business conversion funnel can be enjoyable and plays to our egos. Encountering the Living Christ and moving through a spiritual conversion funnel can be a soul-shaking, ego-smashing journey. The experience for each person moving through the spiritual conversion funnel is different, but we all receive grace. To what extent we let it flow through us and into others is up to us.

The Catholic conversion funnel looks like this:

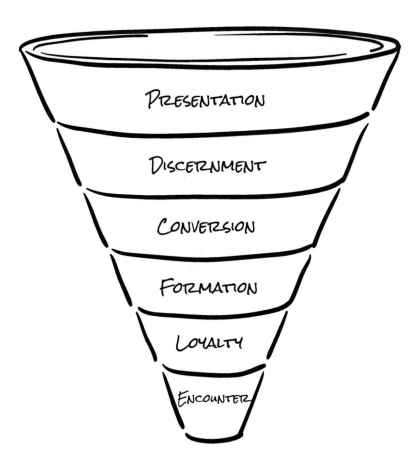

The Bible refers to these stages in many ways. It's valuable to reflect on each not only for our own edification but also to gauge where others are as we interact with them.

Presentation

Ever since the creation of the world, his invisible attributes of eternal power and divinity have been able to be understood and perceived in what he has made. As a result, they have no excuse. (Romans 1:20)

Sometimes I feel discouraged that so many people around me don't know God exists. During these times, I remind myself the Lord makes himself known through the canvas of the universe. His amazing creation fills people with wonder even if people don't see God in it directly, or don't know to look for God. The senses of every person you meet have been overwhelmed by the beauty and mystery of God's creation at least once in their lives. I often find even people who have thrown out the idea of religion are still open to the idea of some power behind the universe.

Indeed, the word of God is living and effective, sharper than any two-edged sword, penetrating even between soul and spirit, joints and marrow, and able to discern reflections and thoughts of the heart. (Hebrews 4:12)

Scripture is more than printed words on a page. The word of God is alive, which means the Holy Spirit uses it to create a unique experience for every individual who reads it with an open heart. This is why many Christian denominations often suggest nonbelievers read the Gospel according to St. John. It's one of the easiest gospels to read because of John's simple presentation of the Good News. It then gives the Holy Spirit a chance to use the Living Word to break down barriers. For Catholics, Scripture is rooted in our daily lives through the liturgy. The Word comes to us in the uniformity of the liturgy given to one people so that we may be continually converted as one people of faith.

We are also living representatives of Jesus Christ through our understanding of the Bible and our frequent reception of the holy Eucharist. God expects us to present the saving power of Christ to everyone we meet. What better way to do this than to literally carry Jesus within us when we consume the holy Eucharist, which provides us a sanctifying grace that allows us to grow spiritually.

People who have seen God's mighty creation develop a natural belief that God is everywhere and in everything. When we carry Jesus with us through the reception of holy Communion, we become more than the canvas. We carry with us the artist who deeply cares about his creation. It is then we become a conduit with which the Holy Spirit can work through, especially to reach those who actively reject Christianity or all forms of religion. This doesn't mean we're required to memorize and quote Scripture at every turn. There will be times that a passage from Scripture will make an important contribution during a conversation. Scripture may even come to us when we face temptations. But it's most important to allow Scripture to cut deep into our souls and transform us from the inside out. People will only be attracted to a Catholic way of life if we are a living example of the transformational power of the Word. Then they might ask what carries us forward each day, and that's our opportunity to help them move into the next phase: discernment.

Discernment

The story of Jesus is the greatest story ever told—an almighty God who humbles himself as a baby and takes upon himself all the sins of humanity. The story of Jesus compels people to confront their own selfishness and sinfulness. The lives of the saints give us mentors in how to live a life like Jesus.

Every person who truly believes in Jesus as our God and Savior has to let go of pride and ego at some point in his or her life. This transition from external to internal belief is what St. Paul referred to when he wrote "work out your salvation with fear and trembling." When and how this initial internalization happens is different for everyone and continues throughout our lives. We have the least influence over others during this part of their conversion. We can only help set up the conditions. To move forward, they must make a personal choice from within the depths of their hearts.

St. John wrote, "the Son of God has come and has given us discernment to know the one who is true" (1 John 5:20). The fact that even our discernment is a gift should encourage us to remain vigilant in our prayers regarding those who have yet to make this personal choice. Even if it seems a person has given up on God, God has not given up on him or her. There is always hope God's love will move someone past discernment and into conversion.

Conversion

So whoever is in Christ is a new creation: the old things have passed away; behold, new things have come. (2 Corinthians 5:17)

Everything about us changes when the walls of pride and ego come crumbling down and we hand our lives over to God. The Holy Spirit fills us. We become one with our fellow believers. The light of Jesus Christ shines in and through us. There are two types of conversions in our lifetime: the first, and all the ones after that. Perhaps the friends on your list grew up in the faith and made the decision to believe in

Jesus alongside their peers. The Church has sacramentalized this in the form of confirmation, a liturgical rite that occurs when we are at the age of discernment. The Church says we are ready to make a decision and gives us the opportunity to do so as a community. No doubt there are many who internalize this decision and are converted from the inside out because of the grace conferred through the sacrament. But I expect there are just as many, if not more, who go through the motions because it's just what they're supposed to do, rather than making it a truly personal choice.

Conversion is only a starting point. I often wish that perfect light of Jesus Christ that shines during conversion would permanently scatter my sins and I would become perfect, as our heavenly Father is perfect. However, usually the opposite is true. A window looks deceptively perfect when seen in the dark, much like my selfish and self-centered ego will convince me I'm perfect when I'm really in the darkness of sin. The imperfections of the window, like me, can only be seen when exposed to light. My character flaws and sins show up as black stains across the window and prevent the full power of Christ to shine through until I repent and seek forgiveness. Daily conversion should inspire us to start scrubbing away the sins that hold us back. The sudden observance of sins and a desire to change is a sign your friends have experienced a conversion. Quickly step in and give them guidance and formation before they become complacent.

Formation

But solid food is for the mature, for those whose faculties are trained by practice to discern good and evil. (Hebrews 5:14)

Conversion is a 7-11 Big Gulp of Jesus on a scorching summer day. It provides fantastic relief, but it doesn't last. We'll begin to crave more than a momentary quenching of our thirst. Coming to believe in Jesus Christ is only the start of the journey. This thirst for more will spur our friends to go out and learn more.

What I love most about our Catholic faith is its depth. The smartest person alive could dive into its mysteries and never find the bottom. There are new experiences and ample knowledge to enlighten and challenge us, including Bible studies, *Lectio Divina*, Mass, Catholic books, the mysteries of the rosary, the Eucharist, the lives of the saints, theology, apologetics, homilies, history, the *Catechism*, retreats, Catholic conferences, and so much more. All of these options give our minds one thing to chew on—truth.

They strengthened the spirits of the disciples and exhorted them to persevere in the faith, saying, "It is necessary for us to undergo many hardships to enter the kingdom of God." (Acts 14:22)

Truth is not always easy to digest and there will be times when our friends will have to wrestle with it like Jacob wrestled with God. Thankfully, they have us. Just like any meal, truth is best when shared with others. I don't recommend letting them dine alone. During formation, it is paramount that we surround them so we are formed by truth together. The Church offers formal processes such as the RCIA for those first becoming Catholic and faith formation to guide children toward confirmation. The United States has also seen a lot of emphasis being placed on adult faith formation. Many good Catholic organizations are producing content for Catholics of all types and in all stages of their journey. (You can get started by checking out the resource section of **YouAretheCatholicBrand.com**.)

One thing to mention, it is entirely possible to become so enamored with the cornucopia of Catholic Christian entrees that our friends will forget what brought them to the table in the first place. A human can go more than a month without food but only days without water. This is also true in the spiritual life. I have found myself sometimes surrounded by the good things of faith but light years from Christ. During these times, I must return to the well. Thankfully the well will never run dry for me or for you, no matter how many times we find ourselves crawling back to it hobbled by sin.

Formation is communal, which means it requires an invitation. We can't force someone to convert and grow in faith, but we can invite him or her to join us. This invitation is called evangelization.

Evangelization

Go, therefore, and make disciples of all nations,
baptizing them in the name of the Father, and of the
Son, and of the holy Spirit. (Matthew 28:19)

Evangelization isn't just personalized for the individual on the receiving end, but its delivery is unique to each of us as well. The Church provides an unchanging foundation that we can point to, but we must remember that each person will experience the same truths in different ways. When we evangelize, we invite others into our reality. I am under no illusions that my brand of Catholicism will work for everyone I meet. Compared to all the saints that have come and gone before me, I know very little. Does this make me a poor evangelist? Am I number 2,784,000,294 on the list of all-time evangelists? Nope. I'm number one—just like everyone else. When I share my reality with others, God uses it how he sees fit to guide, to shape, and to mold others on their faith journey. If I am not inviting people into my reality, I'm not evangelizing.

I was surprised and a bit dismayed to learn there was no Bible study for adult men at my new Catholic parish after regularly attending Bible studies for years at a non-denominational church. I had spent those years listening, studying, and occasionally sharing during conversation. I had seen people firsthand who had a deep understanding of Scripture and felt woefully unprepared to lead a men's group myself. In fact, I didn't even try. After I had made a few Catholic friends, I offhandedly asked two of them if they wanted to study the *Catechism* with me, a book about which I was very curious to learn more. I didn't know it at the time, but in that moment God put me in a leadership position.

We aren't meant to stay in the same roles for the eternity of our spiritual journey. God wants us to take our talents and knowledge and invest them in others. That means personalizing our messages and extending unique invitations. The majority of our evangelization will be to strangers in the form of our actions and our restraints. To evangelize to others, we have to encounter them. If you're not sure how to get started, I've included an evangelization chart in the next section that will take the conversion funnel and help you apply it to your reality.

Encounter

Indeed someone may say, "You have faith and I have works."
Demonstrate your faith to me without works,
and I will demonstrate my faith to you from my works. (James 2:18)

And whatever you do, in word or in deed,
do everything in the name of the Lord Jesus,
giving thanks to God the Father through him. (Colossians 3:17)

Jesus understands the human heart. Not only was he there when God created it, but he personally experienced it. The best way for faith to journey from the mind to the heart is through action. It's not enough to say we believe. We have to put our faith into practice. When we evangelize, we are evangelized; just as when we forgive, we are forgiven.

Pope Francis has often used the word *encounter*. Consider this quote:

[F]aith can only be communicated through witness, and that means love. Not with our own ideas but with the Gospel, lived out in our own lives and brought to life within us by the Holy Spirit.... It's not so much about speaking, but rather speaking with our whole lives: living consistently, the very consistency of our lives! This consistency means living Christianity as an encounter with Jesus that brings me to others, not just as a social label....

In this "stepping out" it is important to be ready for encounter.... we must create a "culture of encounter", a culture of friendship, a culture in which we find brothers and sisters, in which we can also speak with those who think differently, as well as those who hold other beliefs, who do not have the same faith. (18 May, 2013)

Pope Francis says Christianity is an encounter with Jesus that brings us to others. The great gift of salvation was given to us despite the fact we are in no way worthy of it. This should inflame our hearts to go out and share the faith with others. Jesus came for us so we must go share him with others. We are here for people, especially those who have been tossed aside and forgotten.

Evangelization Chart

Before we can personalize our message, we have to understand what influence we have. As people move down the chart, our level of influence increases, but so does our responsibility. Every person in our life, no matter how briefly we encounter them, falls into one of the tiers of the evangelization chart. The chart below will help you make sense of it all, and give you some actions to get started. The first column represents the various people in our lives. The second column represents the layer of the funnel they are currently in. The third and fourth column give examples of how we can influence them through our actions.

WE AREN'T MEANT TO STAY IN THE SAME ROLES FOR THE ETERNITY OF OUR SPIRITUAL JOURNEY.

PEOPLE	THEIR FUNNEL LAYER	OUR ACTIONS	ACTION DESCRIPTION
Strangers	All Layers	Deeds, Openness	How we act and what we avoid doing. Stay awake; be ready for God moments.
Acquaintances	Presentation/ Evangelization	Let them know you're Catholic	If someone knows you're a fan of a certain sports team, they should also know you're Catholic
	Encounter	Compassion	Show them the love of Christ
Familiar	Presentation/ Evangelization	Invite them to Mass, dinner, bible study, coffee etc.	Make it known you want to spend more time with them in a spiritual setting
	Discern	Listening	Learn more about their spiritual condition
	Encounter	Random acts of kindness	Expect nothing in return
Close	Presentation/Discern	Tell them your witness	Not just once but every time the Spirit moves you
	Formation	Edification	Teach them the truth even if it conflicts with their lifestyle
	Evangelization	Spend time together	Invite them to dinner or family functions where your faith, lived in the real world, will be on display
	Encounter	Meaningful action	Let them know you are praying for their specific situation or help them based on their needs
Intimate	Presentation/Discern	Answer their questions	Be brave enough to disclose personal details about your struggles in life and in faith
	Formation	Discipleship	Walk with them on their spiritual journey
	Evangelization	Pray together	Invite them to join you in prayer
	Encounter	Walk in their shoes	Empathize with them

Now it's your turn. Use the chart below to name specific people in each category, identify what layer of the conversion funnel they're in, and choose an action you find appropriate. If you don't know what layer they're in, your action can be to speak with them and find out.

CATEGORY	PEOPLE	THEIR FUNNEL LAYER	OUR ACTIONS
Acquaintance			
Familiar			
Close			
Intimate			

It is important to note that conversion is an internal process. More often than not, you won't know where someone is unless you ask. Only a handful of people are far enough down the evangelization chart for a question like that. Even those who feel comfortable enough to answer may not have a true sense of what God is doing in their lives. Remember, each person must work out his or her salvation on their own. Those two foreboding words "fear and trembling" don't seem appropriate for falling in love with an all-loving creator, but to accept the Good News of Jesus Christ is to admit our brokenness, realize we are doomed without a Savior, and then to turn to him completely and ask for our sins to be forgiven. As Catholics, it also means facing any fears or resentments toward the Church and possible cultural backlash. We may never see the fruits of our labor for others, but the Holy Spirit will continue our good work.

> TO ACCEPT THE GOOD NEWS OF JESUS CHRIST IS TO ADMIT OUR BROKENNESS.

If you have worked in the corporate world, you know the demands for performance. Big brands spend billions of dollars each year because they can show something for it—new customers, new markets, and increased profits. A businessperson must show a return on investment. If I wasn't proving my value every day to the clients and companies who hired me, they'd be moving on.

When Jesus told Peter, an expert fisherman, to put out into the deep waters for a catch, Jesus expected to see results. Jesus knew that God's power would bring the greatest results possible. The best managers and visionaries empower the people around them to be successful. They expect success and provide the tools to achieve it.

That's exactly what God has done for us. In the Catholic Church, we have everything we need to be successful. We have Jesus fully present in the Eucharist, the Holy Spirit to guide us and work behind the scenes on our behalf, an apostolic succession back to Peter, the sacraments, Mary the Mother of God and the communion of saints to intercede on our behalf, the liturgy rooted in Scripture, guardian angels, sacramentals, and much more. It's all there. We're not lacking for anything.

But does God expect us to achieve results? It's a fair question, one that I often ask myself. It reminds me of the parable of the talents in the Gospel according to St. Matthew, Chapter 25. Jesus tells the disciples the Kingdom of God is like a master who gives a talent to each worker and then leaves. Upon the master's return, he collects what is due. The first worker turned one into ten, the second worker turned one into four, but the last worker buried his one talent out of fear. The Lord considered the third worker's actions having no value and he is referred to as the "useless servant" (Matthew 25:30).

> **How SUCCESSFUL WE ARE DOESN'T MATTER. GOD JUST WANTS US TO TRY, AND KEEP TRYING.**

But the master's pleasure with both the first two workers, despite the disparity in achievement, was equal. Unlike our worldly bosses, our heavenly one doesn't care how successful we are, just that we try.

This parable speaks to all who have received the Good News. We must not bury it, but give it away, having faith it will increase in value. We have a responsibility to be intentional about how we develop our personal Catholic brand. I'm convinced that the first worker was probably ten times happier than the third worker. In this manner, we will receive earthly rewards for our heavenly work.

Have you ever started a new job, perhaps one where your responsibility was greatly increased? It's a nerve-racking position. Many people pass up promotions out of fear. If you have gone through it, you know that over time it becomes easy, even second nature. But first you have to walk through a period of discomfort. That's how it should be as you develop your personal Catholic brand. Your evangelization chart should never be stagnant. God is too dynamic for that. In one month, six months, or one year, look at the names on your list and ask yourself these questions:

- HAVE I GONE OUT OF MY WAY TO SHOW THEM CHRISTIAN LOVE?

- HAVE I ASKED THEM ABOUT THEIR SPIRITUAL CONDITION?

- HAVE I RELATED MY OWN PERSONAL EXPERIENCE WITH GOD?

- DO I KNOW MORE ABOUT THEM NOW THAN I DID THEN?

If you can answer yes to each of those questions you've done your part. Now God is doing his. If they haven't moved down the sheet, don't worry. Be patient. If your answer is no for one or all of the above questions, ask yourself why. Is it out of fear? Is it the same fear as the man who buried his talent?

The Holy Spirit provides the power to change hearts and lead souls to Christ. We are the conduits of this power. We can easily turn people off or lead them down the wrong path. What actions can we take to make sure our steps are in the right direction? I call this maintaining our Catholic brand.

Chapter
Five

Maintain Your
Catholic Brand

Our Catholic brand isn't about

being perfect;

it's about picking ourselves up

from under our crosses.

At this point, you have a spiritual mission state-ment, a list of friends, and a personalized message. All you need to do is maintain your Catholic brand.

After leaving Crosby Marketing, I landed a job as vice president of interactive marketing at The Bozzuto Group, a regional real estate company. It is a privately held, family-owned business. The owner, Tom Bozzuto, started the business with a couple partners and a few properties twenty years earlier. During that time he and his partners added over 120 properties to their property management division, many of which Bozzuto held ownership stake in.

Tom is a savvy businessman and a natural when it comes to maintaining his company brand. His strong Catholic faith helped shape the vision for his company and rooted it in high ideals such as integrity and honesty. The final line of the company's mission statement reads, "Perfection is a goal worth pursuing."

Every Friday, Tom would drive around doing property visits. I had the opportunity to join him once and watch firsthand as Tom worked to maintain the Bozzuto brand. As we got closer to the property, he would look for way-finding signs. He reasoned that if people can't figure out where to park, they would be quick to go somewhere else. After parking, Tom paused to review everything from the bushes to the sidewalks. If he found something not quite right or even litter on the ground, the manager would be in for a discussion. Tom took the value of curb appeal seriously.

As we approached the front desk, a young woman behind the counter barely looked up and merely said, "Hello."

"My name is Tom Bozzuto," he responded, which got her attention, "and when a customer comes through the door you should stand and greet them."

The young woman behind the counter rose quickly and apologized. She looked more embarrassed than threatened. Tom commanded a room, but he never used that power to demean others. In fact, he began to ask her questions about the property and she recovered well. I could tell she knew her stuff. She'd just been caught being lazy.

The truth is, we're all lazy. Every single one of us. About what and to what degree varies, but we are all predisposed toward the sin of sloth. It's been in our nature ever since Adam and Eve ate the apple, passing original sin on to each of us.

This inclination toward sin is the central theme of the Old Testament. Despite all the warnings from prophets and all the consequences of their actions, the Israelites continued to stray from God's path again and again. As I read through the Old Testament, it became maddeningly clear. The human race is doomed to repeat the same mistakes. Just when they seemed to get their act together, I would flip the page and read so and so begot so and so and he did evil in the sight of the Lord. Each morning on the commuter train when I read through the Old Testament, I wanted to shout, "Seriously? You're going to do that again?!"

The trials of the Israelites, though they occurred historically over the course of centuries and through many generations, are also very much a metaphor for our internal spiritual life. We can never quite get our act together completely. Even when we do, our pride kicks in and we find ourselves slacking off or repeating the same mistakes. The Israelites needed a Savior and so do we.

> THE TRUTH IS, WE'RE ALL LAZY. EVERY SINGLE ONE OF US.

Jesus spoke often of this predisposition towards sinful behavior and warned against it. In Matthew 24:43 he says, "Be sure of this: if the master of the house had known the hour of night when the thief was coming, he would have stayed awake and not let his house be broken into." In Matthew 12:43–45, Jesus speaks of an unclean spirit that after being cast out returns to an empty house and brings more of his demonic friends. Had the watchman been awake, neither the thief nor the spirit would have been able to enter the house.

The moment we stray from the path of virtue and holiness we open ourselves up to damaging ourselves and others. Consequences for brands that stray from their mission statement might include lost customers or revenue, but consequences for us when we stray from virtue, as representatives of the Catholic brand, are much greater. You are a living representative of Christ to the people you meet. You aren't just a celebrity on TV or some vague negative notion of the Church from a random blog or online comment. You may be the only experience of Christ someone has, and because of that your brand is eternally important.

As Catholics, saying one thing but doing another can cause the people we're trying to evangelize to turn away from God. Our actions have serious consequences and we can't take them lightly. However, knowing the consequences doesn't give us the power to choose righteousness over sin. So how can we maintain our brand as genuine followers of Christ?

During my time as leader of the men's group, I fell off the wagon and took a drink after six and half years sober. At the time, I felt as though I couldn't open up to the men in the group because I was in a leadership position. Wasn't I supposed to have it all figured out? My pride held it secret for months, hurting my Catholic brand. I finally came clean after some convincing from the Holy Spirit. Instead of being judged and tossed out of the group, the men surrounded me and helped in so many ways.

I'm an imperfect person who has and will continue to make mistakes. My personal Catholic brand will never be perfect, and neither will yours. Luckily, our Catholic brand isn't about being perfect. It's about continuing to pick yourself up from under the weight of your cross, just as Jesus did. Everyone struggles, and when people see you continue in spite of struggles your Catholic brand becomes more authentic.

Thankfully, Jesus knew this when he gave us the command to be perfect. Which is why Jesus also gave us a formula to follow in the Lord's Prayer.

Our Father Who Art in Heaven, Hallowed Be Thy Name

The Lord's Prayer speaks in the plural form, not the singular. We aren't meant to walk this path alone. God knows there is power in numbers. "We" can do together what "I" cannot do alone. Support from the Body of Christ is essential to maintaining our individual brand. Christians are one in body but still unique individuals. By invoking the holy name of God, we become empowered to place God and others ahead of selfish desires.

The Lord's Prayer starts with a call to humility, which means having two feet planted firmly on the ground. We aren't puffed up above others, but we're not sunken below their feet either. Humility is a right understanding of ourselves in relation to God. God is in heaven and heaven is perfect, and that's where our help comes from. Yes, Jesus commanded us to be perfect despite our fallen world, but he offers us perfect help from above. That help comes in the form of a father who loves us, not a teacher who grades us. A father who nurtures, forgives, and cares about our everyday struggles. A father who meets us where we are.

(Heaven) Does not refer to a place but to God's majesty and his presence in hearts of the just. Heaven, the Father's house, is the true homeland toward which we are heading and to which, already, we belong. (CCC 2802)

Thy Kingdom Come, Thy Will Be Done on Earth as It Is in Heaven

Jesus Christ is the only person to embody a perfect personal Catholic brand. He did this by fully accepting and carrying out the will of God. The Kingdom of God on Earth came with Jesus's arrival and will end when he returns again. To seek the will of God on earth is to ask for the second coming of Christ.

God's will and our personal Catholic brand exist in the present moment. Regret and pride live in the past and worry in the future—both of which are the devil's playground. Yesterday is gone and tomorrow never comes. Today is all we are promised and God wants us to get busy!

We become living billboard signs as we pursue Jesus's command for perfection. People around us won't become attracted to us, but to heaven here on earth. Heaven is the ultimate goal. It's what every human soul longs for. Others should get a glimpse of the destination in our eyes and through our lives. Then they'll want to follow us.

Give Us This Day Our Daily Bread

Refers to our earthly nourishment necessary for life and also the Bread of Life, the Word of God and Body of Christ. (CCC 2861)

As Catholics, we draw our life from the Eucharist each time we receive holy Communion. Just before Jesus left this earth, he promised to be with us every day. Jesus is truly present to us in this divine sacrament, because he is the Bread of Life.

Again, note the plural form of this prayer. We must both give and receive help from others. This is a great spiritual axiom. I need to help you with your personal Catholic brand in order for me to maintain mine. When we retreat into ourselves, convince ourselves that we don't need anyone else or that we have nothing to offer, that's when we have lost our way. Our work as Catholic Brand Evangelists is never over. If I sense I've reached a plateau, then I need to go back through the process starting with my spiritual mission statement. Getting uncomfortable when you've found a place of spiritual comfort is never easy. Jesus knows this, and that's why he offers us help to become courageous on a daily basis. We just have to genuinely ask for it. The nourishment I received yesterday will not sustain me today, and tomorrow may never come. Praying for "our daily bread" is asking God to completely change your life. So watch out!

Forgive Us Our Trespasses as We Forgive Those Who Trespass Against Us

Forgiveness is spiritual Neosporin. If we hold on to resentments, we will live a life filled with anger, hatred, and the desire for retaliation. This results in endless emotional pain. Holding onto a resentment is like drinking poison and hoping someone else dies. All it does is fill us with bitterness and prevent us from living in the way God has planned for us. When we forgive, we're healed from the inside out. Then our personal Catholic brand shines bright with the love of God for all to see. The healing of my marriage began when Shannon forgave me. If she hadn't, we would have been stuck within the ice cold confines of anger and shame.

This forgiveness should also be extended from ourselves to ourselves. Often the person I hold the most resentment towards is myself. I feel shame and guilt over my past and present sins. I learned, like St. Paul who called himself the foremost of sinners, that I need to admit I'm a sinner first. Once I acknowledge my sins, especially in the sacrament of reconciliation, it opens me up to receive the grace of forgiveness from God. If simple human forgiveness heals the spirit, imagine the effect of heavenly forgiveness!

Sometimes I find myself taking out the worn-out bat that is shame and guilt, beating myself up over past sins. No one is harsher to me than me. During those moments I must remember that God came to earth as a man to pay the price for my sins. If I'm truly repentant and seek forgiveness through reconciliation, who am I to hold resentments against myself when God has already forgiven me?

Lead Us Not Into Temptation But Deliver Us From Evil

When we pray this line we aren't asking God to remove all temptation from our lives. Instead, we are asking for his strength to resist the temptations that come, and the guidance to build our Catholic brand. Each day we give our broken selves to God and, in turn, he gives us back a personal brand better than anything we could create on our own.

Maintaining our personal Catholic brand has one underlying principle—action. Living the spiritual life is an eternal task. We never reach the goal of perfection, but we do make progress.

Many companies now employ brand managers. The chief job of the brand manager is to protect, maintain, and extend the brand. One of the best ways to do this is through brand programs. Southwest's Bags Fly Free, Ritz Carlton's Customer Focus, Macy's Return Policy, and on and on. These are focused efforts to reinforce some aspect of the brand ideal by knowing who the customer is and what matters most to them. At Eaves apartments, we developed a "clean sweep" program that allowed renters to pay a little extra up front to safeguard against losing their deposit for an unclean apartment at the end of their lease. This was a direct result of customer research and matched the brand personality of ease, comfort, and doing "a little extra."

Just as the saints are keenly aware of their imperfections, no brand manager is ever happy. From a customer's perspective, you may think brands like Apple or Nike have it all together. But behind each is a team of brand managers pulling their hair out. The best day of a brand's life is when it arrives on paper. Everything makes sense. All the pieces are in perfect harmony. Then life happens. Then people happen.

Brand programs are as much for employees as they are for customers. It's crucial employees buy into the brand and are knowledgeable about what it stands for. All it takes is one poor experience with a baggage handler, hotel clerk, or customer returns agent for the whole thing to fall apart.

In recent years, many brands have been investing heavily in learning and development teams as part of human resources. These folks are charged with developing learning modules that help employees continue to improve their brand skills. These modules are designed using the latest adult learning techniques and always include measurable objectives.

Every brand program and every employee's performance is tied to a previously determined customer satisfaction point that relates back to the brand's mission. If the mission is being fulfilled, then the company is growing and is profitable.

Back to my experience with the Bozzuto Group, Tom Bozzuto came across the online reviews for one of his properties and they were horrible. He forwarded me the link and told me to do something about it. This was a stellar property and had high customer satisfaction. The online reviews didn't seem to match reality, and the higher ups wanted it fixed immediately. Unlike hotels, which have customers for an average of two nights, apartment communities have them for an average of eighteen months. All it takes is one bad customer service experience for the branding to fall apart.

I was going to need help from the learning and development team because this problem required a culture change. I sat down with the director and brought her up to speed. She immediately asked how we could measure a change and how it could be tied to employee performance. To be effective, it had to be measurable.

In this scenario, renters were evaluating apartments for a variety of things such as parking, noise, maintenance, schools, neighborhood, and so forth. Some factors we could influence and some were out of our control. So how could we activate our own Brand Evangelists? How could we get employees to buy into this new way of thinking? One word encompassed everything we were trying to accomplish and it came to me only after several brainstorming sessions. "Yes!" It was the answer we needed to strive for in reply to the question, "would you recommend us to family and friends?"

> JUST AS THE SAINTS ARE KEENLY AWARE OF THEIR IMPERFECTIONS, NO BRAND MANAGER IS EVER HAPPY.

If the majority of our customers would be willing to recommend us to the most important people in their lives, the company would be successful. This one question cut through some of the peripheral issues and went straight to the heart of the matter. The Yes! Program was born.

Long before brand programs like Yes!, the Catholic Church had the most powerful brand program of all time—the liturgy. The liturgy is expressed in different ways throughout the world, but its core attributes are the same. If you go to Mass anywhere in the United States, you'll hear the same readings and prayers. Where we often fall short as an institution is the experience before the experience and the experience after the experience. From Google search to holy water, many people have varied and sometimes confusing experiences. websites, welcome efforts, and follow-ups all need better Catholic brand programs to help people feel welcome, connect them to a local community, and shepherd them to a closer relationship with Jesus Christ.

I encourage you to talk with your pastor about implementing some of the ideas in the resource section on my blog. Many are free and they have been proven successful. Be encouraged, many people are working hard at the diocesan and national level to create programs and best practices that will help unify the new parishioner experience.

At the beginning of this book, I said that you are a defender of the Catholic brand. So how can you maintain it? What are the brand programs you can implement in your life? First, go back to your mission statement. You should regularly refer to it and increase or shift your activities in ways that relate back to the areas of strength that you identified.

For example, the final sentence in the mission statement I created for myself—"When given the opportunity, I will evangelize by relating how I grew up Catholic and was fully converted when I struggled with alcoholism."—was the impetus for this book. I experienced firsthand the positive reactions of those I opened up to regarding my struggles with alcoholism as it related to my faith journey. At the same time, I was learning how to construct and maintain brands that would resonate more effectively with customers. I began to wonder if both my personal experience and professional expertise would help other Catholics hone a personal brand they were already exuding. My story is one among millions, each story with its own flavor and learnings. Personal stories create a living, moving brand for the Catholic Church. Personal stories and ministries play to our strengths and relate back to our mission statement. Remember, a brand program is simply a coordinated effort that ties into a goal. That goal is to help each other more fully experience God's presence here on earth and forever in the next.

Another thing big brands do well is knowing where they stand. If brand attributes are formalized into brand programs that relate back to the mission statement, the question becomes, "Is it working?" You may think brands have sophisticated tracking systems for measurement, but often the most successful ones find a simple, easy way to measure effectiveness. In recent years, one simple system called the Net Promotion Score, or NPS, has taken off. The number of brands that have started to use this system is staggering. And the reason is simple. It works. The NPS starts by asking a question, much like the Yes! Program.

"How likely would you be to recommend X to family and friends?"

The response is given on a scale of 1–10, 10 being the most likely. This question allows brands to get to the heart of what matters most, but also track change over time. NPS has the ability to measure overall performance of the brand as well as specific attributes like the breakfast menu, the drive-through window, or the customer service staff.

In the same way, we can also gauge how effectively our evangelization tactics are working. We now know, through the example of NPS, that the act of passing something on to someone is a form of acceptance. I won't hand something off or tell someone about something unless I've bought in myself. If we want to know where we stand

REMEMBER, A BRAND PROGRAM IS SIMPLY A COORDINATED EFFORT THAT TIES INTO A GOAL.

in our evangelization efforts, we need to know how our message is being received. For example, if you're someone who gives out rosaries, prayer cards, or other items, consider giving two. The next time you see that person, ask them if they gave the other one away.

Every Christmas Eve, I invite some of the men at the outer edges of my circle to midnight Mass. I've found it to be very effective. There is something about an invitation to midnight Mass that speaks directly to a spiritual truth. We often make spiritual progress when, as St. John of the Cross said in *Dark Night of the Soul*, our house is at rest. Just as Elijah didn't hear God in the thunder, wind, or fire, but as a whisper, so too it is with us. God moves as deep within us as we let him, but we can block him out with the noise of life. St. Peter describes Satan as a roaring lion prowling around seeking the ruin of souls. Something prowling and hidden, yet roaring and overwhelmingly loud. All that noise can keep us from hearing God's whisper. God waits for moments of calm to make his presence known.

One Christmas Eve I walked into midnight Mass with a Buddhist, a Wiccan, a fallen away Catholic, and a new age spiritualist. Prior to Mass, we met down the street for coffee. (It's important to take five minutes and give visitors a quick overview of what happens in Mass, especially if they have never been before.) As for the Eucharist, I tell them Catholics understand the host truly becomes the Body of Christ and the wine the Blood of Christ. I recommend only those who believe the same go up to receive the Eucharist. I find that approach takes away any chance of being offended or not feeling welcome because they acknowledge they don't share the same belief.

My new age spiritualist friend was quiet throughout Mass. He didn't read or sing along. I was sure that with each passing moment he regretted more and more accepting my invitation.

After Mass, as we said our goodbyes in the parking lot, tears started streaming down his face. He said the idea of God revealing himself not to the high and mighty but to the lowly shepherds in the fields had a profound impact on him. He had heard the Christmas story before but it had never impacted him the way it did that night. He said he had no idea why the significance of the story had never penetrated his soul. I knew though. His house was finally at rest.

An invitation to midnight Mass occurs way outside the pressures of life. Over the years, when I see those men again, I ask if they have been to Mass again or if they have shared that initial experience with family or friends. Gathering this information has been invaluable for my efforts. It has helped me understand how well I'm doing in fulfilling my mission and it has led to new ways of doing things.

Talking with men on the outskirts of Christianity and the Church led me to start a men's group at my parish. We started with just a handful of men meeting every other week in the "upper porch" of my home and it has grown to twenty plus men meeting every week at the parish. Because they "bought in" to this form of mission, this group has since launched another men's group that attracts 75 men or more on a weekly basis.

The idea of creating promoters is nothing new for Christians. It was Jesus's last great commission to go out to all nations and make disciples. Jesus's message would only have lasted a generation if the Good News didn't convert more people into evangelists.

> GOD WAITS FOR MOMENTS OF CALM TO MAKE HIS PRESENCE KNOWN.

Certainly, one of the ways the apostles were able to measure whether or not they were carrying out Jesus's command successfully was the number of disciples they were able to form.

We can't measure our success by the number of converts alone. Belief in Jesus is a gift from God and it comes from the Holy Spirit who empowers us to know what to say and enables the unbeliever to listen with an open heart. What we can measure as success is how often we're allowing the Holy Spirit to work through us.

Discipleship sounds like something from a seminary or evangelical church, but it's not denomination or clergy specific. All Christians should consider themselves disciples of Jesus Christ and discipleship is how that happens. The Catholic Church has formalized the process through the RCIA for adults and faith formation for children. These programs have the potential to mold and shape the next wave of Brand Evangelists. But as a Brand Evangelist, we must not rely solely on the Church. We also need to seek out faithful Catholics who encourage us and who we can encourage.

It is important not to try to "disciple" the whole community. Perhaps the overwhelming idea of the needs of others is what turns most people off from attempting personal discipleship. Remember how Jesus discipled others. He was a preacher to large crowds, but he spent most of his personal time with the twelve apostles. He spent even more time with three in particular—Peter, James, and John. This is why the small group model works, because Jesus invented it. Our Church would be transformed if we all had a small group of men or women that we met with regularly who challenged us to learn more, grow deeper, and live the faith more effectively.

Companies know where they stand in their branding efforts through brand audits. Audits are tedious, but they are vital to the continued health of any organization. Brands are made up of people, and people get complacent. It's the same with our personal lives. How do we ensure maximum effectiveness as a Catholic Brand Evangelist? The best answer relates back to our mission statement. Six months after reading this book, I challenge you to return to this page and complete the audit below. If you have your phone with you, take a few seconds to put a reminder on your calendar.

In six months, you may find that you're right on track, or that there are areas that need more attention, or that circumstances in your life have changed enough to warrant modifying your mission statement.

	No Improvement			Very Improved	
Prayer	1	2	3	4	5
Being open to Holy Spirit	1	2	3	4	5
Spiritual Reading	1	2	3	4	5
Moving past my fears	1	2	3	4	5
Reducing character defects	1	2	3	4	5
Stepping out of my comfort zone	1	2	3	4	5
Assessing people's spiritual position	1	2	3	4	5
Being of service in my strengths	1	2	3	4	5
Improving areas of weakness	1	2	3	4	5

When you get through the audit, you may find that it's time for a "re-brand." Don't be afraid to reinvent yourself. While we must know who we are, and where we are going, we should never stay a course that isn't working for us. Life happens. Things change. Maybe it's a new season in life that has prompted different interests. The prodding of the Holy Spirit occurs in unexpected ways. Staying open to God's will means your life is not your own and you shouldn't get too attached to the status quo.

In the business world, it often takes a consulting firm's perspective to identify and make the necessary changes to respond to the market. People get so close to their brands that they're unable to see the time has come to make a big, necessary change. Many jobs are lost for this very reason.

Our personal lives are no different. We may be hanging onto a ministry too long, after the signs point to the need to move on. Here, it's best to seek outside counsel. A spiritual director proves invaluable. They visit us on our personal islands and help provide a new, fresh perspective.

Being a Catholic brand evangelist means being uncomfortable, challenged, enlightened, comforted, uplifted, introspective, concerned, and all the other adjectives that mean anything in this life. It is a great privilege and a great responsibility to bear the Catholic brand. Stay open to God's will and surround yourself with other brand evangelists. Most of all, find joy in keeping your eyes fixed on Christ.

Afterword

To download additional copies of the spiritual inventory sheet and evangelization chart go to: **www.YouAreTheCatholicBrand.com**.

To connect with other Catholic Christian Brand Evangelists and to share your personal stories, join the conversation on social media:

Instagram.com/youarethecatholicbrand/

Facebook.com/YouAreTheCatholicBrand

Twitter.com/CatholicBrand

Appendix

Charts and Graphs

Resentment/Fear Inventory Chart (Left Side)

Resentment or Fear	About What? Why?	What Was Affected? (threatened or hurt)					
		Self Esteem	Personal Relations	Marital Security	Emotional Security	Sexual	Ambition
RESENTMENT	CHURCH COVERED UP SEX ABUSES				X		
RESENTMENT	MY PRIEST GROWING UP DID NOT TAKE ME OUT TO LUNCH	X	X				X
FEAR	MY FAMILY WON'T GO TO HEAVEN		X		X		X

Resentment/Fear Inventory Chart (Right Side)

The Exact Nature of Our Wrongs. Where was I?						Where was I to blame?
Selfish	Dishonest	Self-Seeking	Frightened	Ungrateful	Resentful	
			x		x	
x				x		
			x			

Character Defects / Assets Chart

CHARACTER DEFECTS	CHARACTER ASSETS
conceited, self-important, vain	humble, modest
controlling	let go, especially of other's lives
critical	non-judgmental, praising, tolerant,
dishonest	honest
envying	empathetic, generous, admiring
false pride	modest, humble
fantasizing, unrealistic	practical, realistic
fearful	confident, courageous
gluttonous, excessive	moderate
gossiping	closed-mouth, kind, praising
greedy	moderate, generous, sharing
impatient	patient
impulsive, reckless	consistent, considered actions
intolerant	tolerant, understanding, patient
jealous	trusting, generous, admiring
judgmental	broadminded, tolerant
justifying (own actions)	honest, frank, candid
lustful	healthy sexuality
manipulative	candid, honest, non-controlling
over sensitive	emotionally stable
perfectionist	realistic goals
procrastinates	disciplined, acts promptly
rationalizing	candid, honest
resentful	forgiving
self-pity	grateful, realistic, accepting
self-seeking	selfless, concerned for others
selfish	altruistic, concerned with others
ungrateful	thankful, grateful

Spiritual Mission Statement Exercise

God loves me.

1. I grew up _____.
   (CATHOLIC)

2. My faith became my own when I _____.
   (STRUGGLED WITH ALCOHOLISM)

3. Some doubts I have are _____.
   (THAT I CAN SUPPORT MY FAMILY AS AN AUTHOR)

4. Some fears I have are _____.
   (I WILL NOT BE ABLE TO STAY SOBER)

5. Some resentments I have are _____.
   (GOD HASN'T CURED ME OF ADDICTION)

6. Some things I currently do to move past these doubts, fears, and
   resentments are _____.
   (DAILY SCRIPTURE READING, FAMILY ROSARY, HANGING
   OUT WITH MEN OF FAITH.)

7. My spiritual talents include _____.
   (EVANGELIZATION)

8. I have a soft spot for _____.
   (MEN WHO STRUGGLE WITH ADDICTION)

9. I have a hard time understanding or relating to _____.
   (MIDDLE SCHOOLERS AND TEENAGERS)

10. I have the most influence with _____.
    (MEN IN MY CHURCH)

11. I have the least influence with _____.
    (NEIGHBORS)

12. _____ is what I want the most
    from my Catholic faith. (PEACE AND SERENITY)

God loves me.

Personal Mission Statement Exercise

Take your answers from the Spiritual mission statement exercise and fill in the sample personal mission statement below.

To _____ (7) is my primary objective.

I concentrate my efforts on _____ (10)

and _____ (8). But I realize I need to

expand my efforts with _____ (9) and

_____ (11).

I move past my fears and gain strength through

_____ (6). When given

the opportunity, I will evangelize by relating how I grew up

_____ (1) and was fully converted

when _____ (2).

Remembering, each day, that God loves me, I will seek his will in order

to achieve _____ (12).

Marketing Conversion Funnel Example

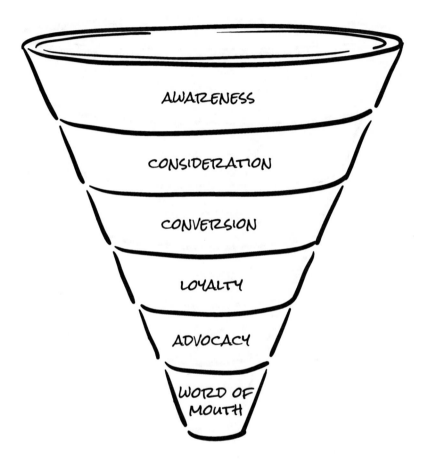

Catholic Conversion Funnel

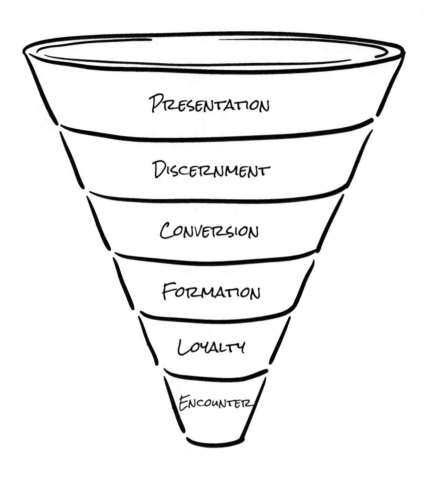

Evangelization Chart

PEOPLE	THEIR FUNNEL LAYER	OUR ACTIONS	ACTION DESCRIPTION
Strangers	All Layers	Deeds, Openness	How we act and what we avoid doing. Stay awake; be ready for God moments.
Acquaintances	Presentation/ Evangelization	Let them know you're Catholic	If someone knows you're a fan of a certain sports team, they should also know you're Catholic
	Encounter	Compassion	Show them the love of Christ
Familiar	Presentation/ Evangelization	Invite them to Mass, dinner, bible study, coffee etc.	Make it known you want to spend more time with them in a spiritual setting
	Discern	Listening	Learn more about their spiritual condition
	Encounter	Random acts of kindness	Expect nothing in return
Close	Presentation/Discern	Tell them your witness	Not just once but every time the Spirit moves you
	Formation	Edification	Teach them the truth even if it conflicts with their lifestyle
	Evangelization	Spend time together	Invite them to dinner or family functions where your faith, lived in the real world, will be on display
	Encounter	Meaningful action	Let them know you are praying for their specific situation or help them based on their needs
Intimate	Presentation/Discern	Answer their questions	Be brave enough to disclose personal details about your struggles in life and in faith
	Formation	Discipleship	Walk with them on their spiritual journey
	Evangelization	Pray together	Invite them to join you in prayer
	Encounter	Walk in their shoes	Empathize with them

Conversion Funnel Assesment

CATEGORY	PEOPLE	THEIR FUNNEL LAYER	OUR ACTIONS
Acquaintance			
Familiar			
Close			
Intimate			

6-Month Branding Audit

	No Improvement			Very Improved	
Prayer	1	2	3	4	5
Being open to Holy Spirit	1	2	3	4	5
Spiritual Reading	1	2	3	4	5
Moving past my fears	1	2	3	4	5
Reducing character defects	1	2	3	4	5
Stepping out of my comfort zone	1	2	3	4	5
Assessing people's spiritual position	1	2	3	4	5
Being of service in my strengths	1	2	3	4	5
Improving areas of weakness	1	2	3	4	5

CPSIA information can be obtained at www.ICGtesting.com
Printed in the USA
LVOW10s2218061016

507755LV00026B/834/P

9 780764 826412